THE
AMERICAN WEST
1840–1895

Mike Mellor

PUBLISHED BY THE PRESS SYNDICATE OF THE UNIVERSITY OF CAMBRIDGE
The Pitt Building, Trumpington Street, Cambridge CB2 1RP, United Kingdom

CAMBRIDGE UNIVERSITY PRESS
The Edinburgh Building, Cambridge CB2 2RU, United Kingdom
40 West 20th Street, New York, NY 10011-4211, USA
10 Stamford Road, Oakleigh, Melbourne 3166, Australia

First published 1998

Printed in the United Kingdom at the University Press, Cambridge

Typeset in Monotype Octavian and FF Meta

A catalogue record for this book is available from the British Library

ISBN 0 521 58633 X paperback

Acknowledgements
We are grateful to the following for permission to reproduce photographs.

Cover: Peter Newark's Western Americana.

Courtesy of the Amon Carter Museum, Fort Worth, Texas: pp. 72 (F.S. Remington, *The Fall of the Cowboy*,
1961.230), 73 (Charles M. Russell, *Cowboy Camp during the Roundup*, # 1961.186), 101 (Charles M. Russell,
In without Knocking, # 1961.201); courtesy of the Anschutz Collection (photo by James O. Milmoe): p. 5;
Arizona State Museum, University of Arizona (photo by Helga Teiwes, # 28883: p. 8; Museum of the North
American Indian, New York/Bridgeman Art Library, London: p. 19; private collection/Bridgeman: pp. 9, 10,
16, 71; Royal Ontario Museum, Toronto/Bridgeman: p. 20; Buffalo Bill Historical Center, Cody, Wyoming:
p. 76; courtesy of the California History Room, California State Library, Sacramento, California: p. 52; courtesy
of the Museum of Church History and Art, used by permission: p. 36*b* (William Warner Major, *Brigham
Young's Family*, © The Church of Jesus Christ of Latter-day Saints); courtesy of the Colorado Historical Society:
pp. 44 (# F12030A), 45 (# F43013), 83 (# WPA 834), 85 (Robert Lindneux); Corbis-Bettmann: pp. 22–23, 69, 100;
Denver Public Library, Western History Department: p. 35; Mary Evans Picture Library: p. 18; Solomon D.
Butcher Collection/Nebraska State Historical Society: pp. 54, 59, 74–75; Peter Newark's Western Americana:
pp. 13, 14, 15*t & b*, 21, 25*t*, *bl & br*, 27, 31, 33, 36*t*, 37, 39, 41, 43, 46–47, 48, 49*t*, 53, 55*t & b*, 57, 58, 61, 63, 65*t & b*,
66*t & b*, 67, 78, 80, 84*t & b*, 88*l & r*, 90, 91, 93, 95, 96–97, 98, 99, 102, 103*t & b*, 104*t & b*, 105*t & b*, 107*t & b*, 108,
109; Rockwell Museum, Corning, New York (photo by James O. Milmoe): p. 11; Smithsonian Institute,
Department of Anthropology: p. 94 (# 55.299); courtesy of the Southwest Museum, Los Angeles: p. 89
(photo ID CT.1 – 1026.G.1); State Historical Society of Wisconsin: p. 56; Texas State Library and Archives
Commission: p. 6.

Picture research by Sandie Huskinson-Rolfe of PHOTOSEEKERS.

Contents

Manifest destiny

The American West covered a vast area from the Mississippi river to the Pacific Coast. It was largely unexplored by white settlers until the beginning of the nineteenth century. In the following decades, many white people from the East Coast went to the West in search of a new life. Much of the land they crossed was made up of mountains, deserts and huge, treeless plains. Going west from the Mississippi to California, there are four main geographical areas, and each of these caused difficulties for those moving from the East:

> First, there are the Great Plains. In the early 1800s, white people thought that this huge area was a barren wasteland that was unsuitable for farming or settlement. They called it the Great American Desert.

> The Rocky Mountains lie west of the Great Plains, and they are almost 200 miles across. At their highest, in Colorado, they are over 14,000 ft.

> The Great Basin and Colorado Plateau is a mixed area of desert, canyons and grasslands ringed by mountain ranges.

> Finally, there are more mountains. The Sierra Nevada range lies before the fertile valleys of California; the Blue Mountains and the Cascades are the last land barriers before the Oregon coast.

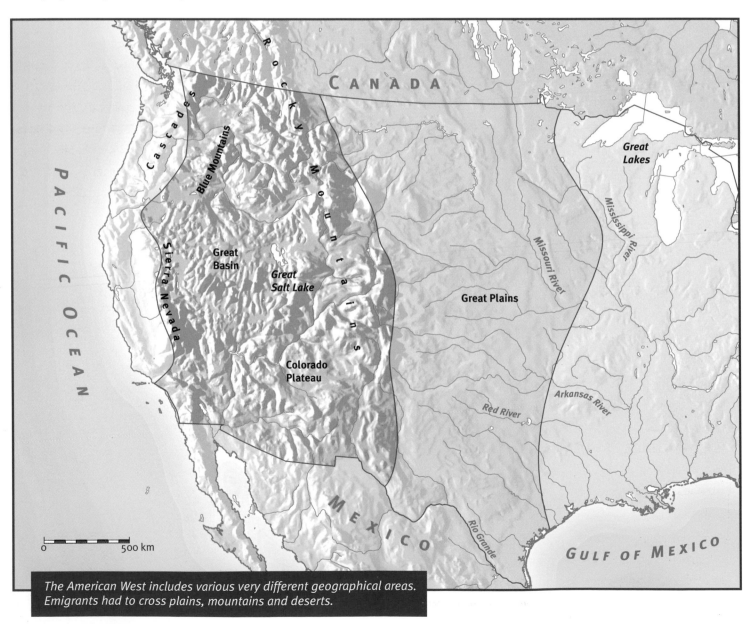

The American West includes various very different geographical areas. Emigrants had to cross plains, mountains and deserts.

Early explorations

The first Europeans to enter the West were the Spanish, who came in from Mexico as early as the sixteenth century. In California, New Mexico and Nevada, many modern place names, for instance San Francisco, Los Angeles and Las Vegas, are Spanish in origin.

When the British came to America, they ignored the West and settled on the East Coast. The first permanent English settlement was founded at Jamestown, Virginia, in 1607. It was not until the end of the eighteenth century that English-speaking Americans began to think about moving west.

One of the first Americans to explore the West was Daniel Boone, later known as the first frontiersman. In 1775, he travelled the Wilderness Road through the Appalachian Mountains into Kentucky. Boone became a legend, and his pioneering spirit encouraged others to think about what lay to the west.

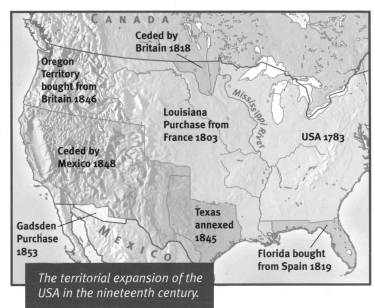

The territorial expansion of the USA in the nineteenth century.

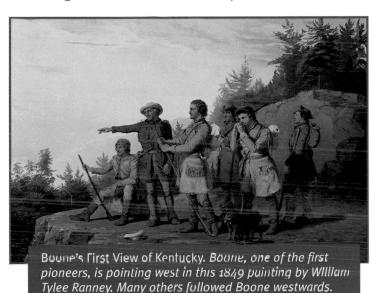

Boone's First View of Kentucky. *Boone, one of the first pioneers, is pointing west in this 1849 painting by William Tylee Ranney. Many others followed Boone westwards.*

How the USA was built up

The US government gradually gained control of the West. The original 13 states along the East Coast won independence from Great Britain in 1783. The USA then included all the land east of the Mississippi apart from Florida, which was finally bought from Spain in 1819.

In 1803, the size of the USA was almost doubled with the Louisiana Purchase. The US government bought the region from France for $15 million when the French ruler Napoleon was mainly concerned with achieving supremacy in Europe. The purchase encouraged white Americans to explore the American continent further.

By the early nineteenth century, many Americans believed that there should be one large American republic stretching from the Atlantic to the Pacific. They thought that this was part of God's plan for the world. In 1845, John L. O'Sullivan, editor of the *Democratic Review*, invented the term 'manifest destiny' to describe what he saw as the USA's God-given mission. He wrote about 'our manifest destiny to overspread the continent allotted by Providence for the free development of our yearly multiplying millions'.

LEWIS AND CLARK

In 1804, the US president Thomas Jefferson wanted the territory west of the Mississippi to be explored and surveyed. Meriwether Lewis and William Clark mounted an expedition that had three main aims:

> to map out the country and undertake a detailed scientific survey;

> to find out if there was a navigable river route to the Pacific;

> to support the growing fur trade by improving relationships with the Native Americans along the Missouri.

Lewis and Clark travelled up the Missouri and reached its head-waters, and then continued on to the Pacific. They collected an enormous amount of information about the native peoples, the land and the wildlife.

Dawn at the Alamo. *This 1905 painting by Henry Arthur McArdle shows the ferocity of the battle.*

Texas and Mexico

In the 1830s, Texas was part of Mexico. Many Texans spoke English and did not wish to be part of a Spanish-speaking country under the Mexican dictator Santa Anna. In 1836, the Texans set up a provisional government in opposition to Santa Anna, and started to fight for their independence.

The best-known episode of this war was the 1836 Battle of the Alamo. The Alamo was a settlement near San Antonio, Texas. Around 200 men, including Davy Crockett, the famous frontiersman, held out there for nearly two weeks against 4000 Mexican troops. The rebels were all killed, but Texas gained its independence just six weeks later. In 1845, Texas joined the USA.

California and Oregon

At the beginning of the nineteenth century, Mexico also controlled California, which then included not only the modern state of California but also Nevada, Arizona and New Mexico. War then broke out between Mexico and the USA in 1846. Overrun by greatly superior numbers, the Mexicans were forced to withdraw, and California became part of the USA in 1848. The modern border between the two countries was settled with the Gadsden Purchase of 1853.

In the early nineteenth century, Great Britain owned the Oregon Territory. In 1846, she offered it to the USA in return for a settlement of the USA–Canada boundary along the 49th Parallel.

By the mid nineteenth century, it seemed that manifest destiny was becoming reality. However, one group of people were deeply unhappy about the white American take-over of the continent: the Native Americans. They had lived in the American West for many centuries before the arrival of the whites.

Discussion points

> How did the US government increase the size of the USA during the first half of the nineteenth century?

> What did white Americans mean when they talked about 'manifest destiny'?

The Native Americans

The distribution of the Native American tribes across North America. The main conflicts with the whites happened on the Great Plains.

When white people began to explore the American West, they found Native Americans (also known as American Indians) living in every part of the region. The Native Americans originally came from northern Asia, and it is thought that they crossed the Bering Straits from Siberia into Alaska using a land bridge formed during the last Ice Age. The first migration is believed to have happened 30,000–40,000 years ago, with the last crossing occurring 10,000 years ago.

Many Native American tribes lived on the Great Plains. The Sioux, the Cheyenne, the Arapaho, the Comanche, the Kiowa and the Kiowa–Apache tribes were particularly important, either because of their numbers or because of the part they played in the history of the West.

INDIAN NATIONS

The Sioux

By the middle of the nineteenth century, there were 25,000–30,000 members of the Sioux nation. The nation was divided into three groups: the Teton (to the west), the Yankton (in the centre) and the Santee (to the east).

Although they were generally known as the Sioux, the members of these tribes called themselves the Lakota (in the Teton dialect), the Nakota (in the Yankton dialect) or the Dakota (in the Santee dialect). Each subgroup was divided into a number of smaller tribes. The Brule, Hunkpapa, Oglala, Blackfeet, Minneconjou, Two Kettle and Sans Arc tribes all belonged to the Teton Sioux.

The Cheyenne

The word 'Cheyenne' is derived from the Sioux term 'Sha hi'e na', meaning 'people speaking language not understood'. The Cheyenne called themselves 'Tsis tsis tas' which means 'the people', or 'ourselves'. They generally got on well with the Sioux, and the two tribes combined to resist the US army in the 1870s.

The Arapaho were allied to the Cheyenne, and they also fought in these campaigns.

The Comanche

The Comanche were known to many whites as the 'lords of the south Plains'. Their high standards of horsemanship and their courage and ferocity in war made them particularly feared opponents, perhaps even more than the Sioux. In 1839, Thomas J. Farnham wrote of 'their incomparable horsemanship, their terrible charge, the unequalled rapidity with which they load and discharge their fire-arms and their insatiable hatred'.

The Kiowa and Kiowa–Apache were closely allied to the Comanche.

The Spanish introduced the horse to the Native Americans. These wall paintings of Spanish horsemen are thought to be by Dibé Yázhí Nééz (Tall Lamb), a Navaho Indian from Arizona.

Unity and diversity

Although all the Great Plains nations and tribes had their own characteristics, they also had much in common:

> Most were hunters, and their ways of life were transformed by the introduction of horses and guns to the Great Plains. They relied heavily on the buffalo for food, clothing and tools.

> Success in warfare was highly prized. Battle rituals were important.

> Their religious beliefs centred on the worship of nature. The religious rituals of the various groups were similar, and they often included symbolic dances and the activities of holy men. The Native Americans believed that the land belonged to everyone.

Discussion points

> How did the Native Americans come to settle in the American West?

> Which were greater, the similarities or differences between the various Native American tribes of the Great Plains?

The importance of the buffalo

Before the whites came to the Great Plains, Native American life revolved around the hunting of the buffalo (more correctly known as the bison). At the beginning of the nineteenth century, enormous herds of buffalo (most historians estimate the numbers to be about 60 million) could be found all over the Great Plains. By the mid-1880s, they were almost extinct, having been hunted by white Americans for their hides and tongues in the full knowledge that their disappearance would threaten the way of life of the Plains Indians.

Why was the buffalo so important to the Plains Indians?

The ancestors of many of the Plains Indians were farmers who grew crops. The Sioux, Cheyenne, Arapaho and many other Native American peoples originally lived in eastern woodland settlements, but the coming of the whites drove them on to the Great Plains during the second half of the eighteenth century. They largely abandoned farming in favour of hunting and a nomadic lifestyle.

The Plains Indians hunted a wide variety of creatures, not just for food, but also for skins to use in clothing and bones to make into equipment. The antelope was a plentiful source of meat, and its hide was used to make garments. Black bear, elk and smaller animals such as beaver and rabbit were also hunted. However, it was the buffalo which was absolutely central to the way of life of the Plains Indians and the successful continuation of their tribal culture.

SOURCE A

Buffalo Hunt *by George Catlin shows the Plains Indian command of their horses and weapons.*

Hunting the buffalo

The life of the Plains Indians mainly depended on two animals: the buffalo and the horse. Horses had been introduced into America by the Spanish. The horse-riding Plains Indians learned to cover vast distances at great speed in pursuit of the buffalo. Their skill with traditional weapons such as the lance and the bow and arrow made them formidable hunters.

SOURCE B

George Catlin was an artist and explorer who studied and lived among the Plains Indians. He described how the Native Americans hunted animals with bows, arrows and lances:

They are almost literally always on their horses' backs, and they wield these weapons with desperate effect upon the open plains. On their horses' backs at full speed, they can come alongside of any animal which they easily destroy.

G. Catlin, *North American Indians*, 1841

The buffalo had poor eyesight, and so they were relatively easy targets for accomplished horsemen. Buffalo hunting was a communal activity, and almost everyone had a part to play. Medicine men carried out religious rituals to attract the bison herds. Mounted warriors surrounded the animals, and herded them into funnel-shaped channels called drive lanes. The buffalo were then guided into compounds to be killed, or they were chased over steep cliffs. They plunged to their deaths, or were finished off by the hunters with bows and lances while they were injured and stunned. The women skinned and cut up the animals.

SOURCE C

The artist and writer George Catlin (1796–1872) lived and worked among the Plains Indians. His print Hunt (a surround) *(1844) shows how the buffalo were trapped.*

HOW THE BUFFALO SUSTAINED LIFE

Almost every part of the buffalo was used by the Plains Indians:

> Buffalo meat was the principal food of the Plains Indians. The meat was usually dried and powdered, and it was sometimes mixed with dried berries. This was known as 'pemmican'. The liver and tongue of the buffalo were also eaten.

> Raw buffalo hides were used to make shields, ropes, saddles, moccasins (shoes), buckets and drums. Tepee (tent) covers, robes, bed covers and bags were made of tanned buffalo hide.

> Buffalo stomachs were used as containers, for example for cooking and to store water.

> The bones of the buffalo were used to make spoons, cups, tools, war clubs and ornaments.

> The hooves were used in tool making, and they were boiled down for glue.

> The horns were converted to domestic utensils such as cups and ladles, and they were worn on head-dresses.

> Thread and bow strings were made from buffalo sinews.

> Buffalo hair was used in head-dresses.

> Buffalo dung, known as 'chips', was burned for fuel.

> Even the buffalo's skull was sometimes used in religious ceremonies. The heart, though, was left untouched, in the belief that this would ensure that the buffalo herds would continue to prosper.

The spiritual importance of the buffalo

Thriving buffalo herds were more than a practical necessity. They also had spiritual significance.

SOURCE D

The buffalo was not just used for food. Joseph H. Sharp's Prayer to the Spirit of the Buffalo *(1910) shows a buffalo skull being used in a religious ceremony.*

SOURCE E

A warrior of the northern Plains explained the importance of the buffalo:

The great Father of Life who made us and gave us this land to live on, made the buffalo to afford us sustenance. They are our only means of life – food, fuel and clothing.

Statement at 36th US Congress, 1859–61

>> Activities

1 Draw a spider diagram to show how Native Americans used the horse. Draw another to show how they used the buffalo.

2 Use the spider diagrams to show which animal was more important to the Native Americans.

3 How do Sources D and E in this investigation indicate that the Plains Indians saw the buffalo as more than just a plentiful supply of food?

Native American weapons and warfare

Weapons

The Native Americans found that riding skills and mastery of the bow and lance were essential, not only for hunting but also for war. They made bows and arrows out of the highest-quality wood available, such as yew or ash. A lance had a tip of sharpened flint or bone, and it was used like a bayonet or javelin. A warrior's decorated shield meant a great deal to him, and it was often buried with him after his death.

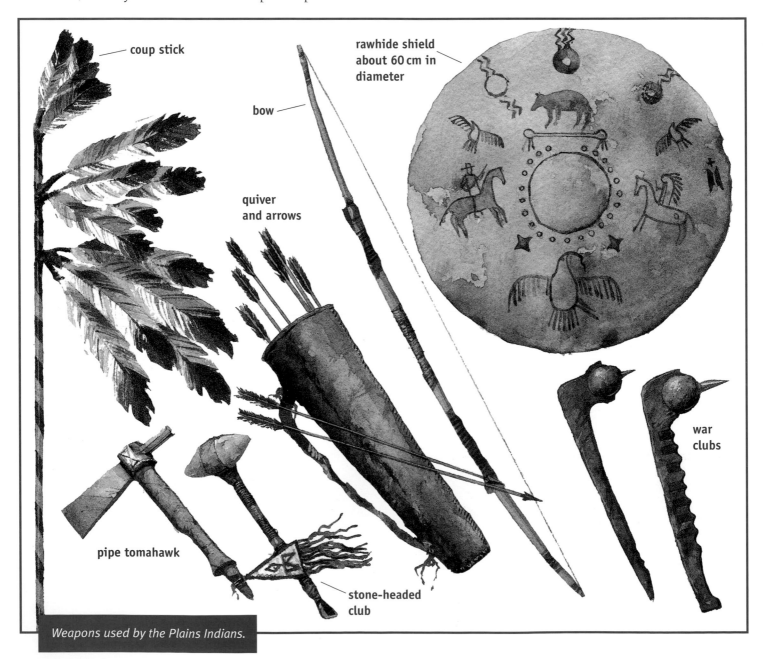

coup stick

bow

rawhide shield about 60 cm in diameter

quiver and arrows

war clubs

pipe tomahawk

stone-headed club

Weapons used by the Plains Indians.

A Crow Chief on Horseback, *drawn by George Catlin.*
Both horse and rider have highly decorated head-dresses.

Warfare

Success in war was of great importance to the Plains Indians, both for individual warriors and for the tribe as a whole. They went to war not to conquer other tribes or to acquire land (because they were nomadic, there was no need to seize land), but because it was a matter of honour to be a victorious warrior. Individual courage and bravery were what mattered. Their concern for honour was shown by the type of war which they fought. This consisted mainly of inter-tribal rivalry and fierce short battles before the coming of white armies to the Great Plains.

Certain warfare rituals were of great significance. One of these was the practice of 'counting coup'. This consisted of running or galloping up to the enemy at high speed and touching him with the end of a 'coup stick'. This was a pole decorated with feathers that was 8–10 ft long. The ritual was an example of the importance of honour, because it was considered far more noble to confront your opponent at close range than from a distance. A warrior gained points for counting coup, and these gave him status within his tribe. Coups had to be verified by witnesses, and they were ceremonially recorded after each battle.

Many tribes cut off the scalps (the skin and hair on top of the head) of their dead enemies. The acquisition of a scalp conferred great prestige on a warrior, and he hung his scalps in a prominent place on a pole in his tepee or on his horse. Scalping may seem barbaric today, but it was also practised by white people in the West.

The treatment of prisoners of war by the Plains Indians varied greatly. Terrible atrocities could be committed, and the Comanche had the most fearsome reputation. Women and children, though, were often treated mercifully and accepted into the victorious tribe.

Discussion point

> Many white Americans thought that the fact that Native American warriors sometimes scalped their dead enemies proved that Native Americans were 'savages'. Was this a fair opinion?

Life among the Plains Indians

White people saw the Plains Indians as savages, but in fact each Native American tribe had a complex culture and social structure of its own. Each group had a strong sense of identity.

What was life like for the Plains Indians?

Social organisation and government

Each tribe was organised into bands of 100–500 people. These groups usually consisted of several large families. Each band was headed by a chief, who was chosen by warriors. He was usually a wise and respected older member of the band who had distinguished himself in war. A council of elders, presided over by the chief, judged disagreements, made arrangements for ceremonies, and generally kept order through the soldier braves.

In some of the larger tribes, such as the Sioux and the Cheyenne, the chiefs of all the bands had to meet when particularly important decisions had to be made. The Cheyenne were led by a council of 44 chiefs. Decisions about war were normally made by special war chiefs.

SOURCE B

George Grinnell, a white man who made several detailed studies of the Cheyenne, wrote about the role of the chief:

A good chief gave his whole heart and his whole mind to the work of helping his people, and strove for their welfare with an earnestness and a devotion rarely equalled by the rulers of other men.

G. Grinnell, *The Cheyenne Indians: Their History and Ways of Life,* 1923

Land and ownership

The Plains Indians did not believe that areas of land should be owned by individuals or families. Tribal homelands belonged to the people as a whole, and there was a strong sense of community. This stemmed from the belief that human beings were indivisible from all the other elements of the natural world: animals, birds, soil, air, mountains, water and the sun. Everything was linked and essential for survival. The earth was something that belonged to everyone, and it was therefore unnatural to claim or buy land.

SOURCE A

Sioux Indian Council, *painted by Seth Eastman in about 1849.*

The tepee

Families lived in tepees, or lodges, which were large conical tents constructed of buffalo hides sewn together and hung on four main poles.

The tepee's focal point was a fire in the middle of the floor, around which were arranged the family's beds. The interior of the tent was decorated with skins, furs and rugs, and colourful religious symbols often adorned the outside.

SOURCE C

Karl Bodmer's Sioux Village *(1833). The tepees were made of buffalo hide.*

SOURCE D

Seeking New Hunting Grounds *by Charles M. Russell (1891) shows how the travois was used to move the tepees.*

SOURCE E

In 1853, Randolph B. Marcy, a white visitor to a Wichita village in present-day Oklahoma, described the tepees:

Twenty-five feet in diameter at the base, twenty feet high, and in the distance have very much the appearance of a group of hay-stacks.

A. Debo, *A History of the Indians of the United States*, 1970

As the Native Americans moved frequently from hunting ground to hunting ground, they had to be able to dismantle the tepees quickly and transport them easily. The lodge poles (each tepee had about 25 of these) and the tepee coverings were moved by means of a 'travois', which was a horse-drawn sledge that was itself made from lodge poles. A disadvantage of the travois was that it was cumbersome, slow-moving and easy to attack.

Family life

Most marriages were monogamous (that is, a man was married to only one woman at a time). In some tribes, polygamy (where a man has more than one wife) was practised. Amongst other things, polygamy was a way of protecting widows and their children. Women widowed after the deaths of their husbands in battle could marry a man who already had a wife.

Most marriages were arranged between the families.

SOURCE F

Often, the young people had already shown an interest in each other by the time marriage was discussed:

Once a boy has seen a girl whom he hopes to make his sweetheart, he approaches her furtively. He knows the path from her family lodge to the stream where she gets water or the grove where she gathers wood. Hopefully, he stands along the path. As she passes, he gives her robe a little tug. If all goes well, they may later begin to meet and talk outside her lodge. In time they may exchange rings. They are then engaged.

E. Adamson Hoebel, *The Cheyennes*, 1978

Within the family, men and women had clearly defined roles, and they had traditional responsibilities within marriage. A man's main duty was to hunt for food. The women skinned the animals and prepared the food, made the clothes, the tepee covers and household goods, and brought up the children. They were also expected to gather items such as water, wood and berries, and to take charge of the packing and unpacking as families moved from camp to camp. In short, women looked after almost all aspects of domestic life.

SOURCE G

This print by George Catlin shows Comanche women dressing buffalo hides.

Children were prepared for their roles from an early age. Boys were trained to hunt and taught about war. They were shown how to ride a horse almost as soon as they could walk. Use of the bow and arrow came shortly afterwards.

SOURCE H

Black Elk was a holy man of the Oglala Sioux. He was a second cousin of the famous warrior Crazy Horse. In his life story, he recollected his childhood:

All the boys from five or six years up were playing war. The little boys would gather together from the different bands of the tribe and fight each other with mud balls that they threw with willow. And the big boys played the game called Throwing-Them-Off-Their-Horses, which is a battle all but the killing; and sometimes they got hurt.

Black Elk, *Black Elk Speaks,* 1932

From the age of three or four, girls learnt how to perform household tasks with their mothers. They helped to collect wood, water, berries, fruit and nuts, and as they got older they learned how to cook, prepare hides and set up tepees. Girls also learned how to ride, although they did not spend as long in the saddle as boys. Both girls and boys played with balls and hoops, and girls were given dolls and cradles.

Old people were well cared for and respected, although mischievous boys might play tricks on groups of elderly men. In turn, old people respected the needs of their tribe, and did not want to be a burden to others. Sometimes they even went off into the plains to die alone.

>> Activities

1 Describe the everyday life of the Plains Indians.

2 Many white Americans called the Native Americans 'uncivilised'. Do you agree? Use your answer to the first question to help you decide.

Native American religion and beliefs

The white Americans were Christians, and most of them did not take Native American beliefs seriously. In fact, though, the Plains Indians had a complex system of religious ideas.

What did the Plains Indians believe in?

SOURCE A

A medicine mask dance painted by Paul Kane (1810–71).

Interconnection

The Plains Indians believed that the land was sacred. All the elements of the natural world were connected, and should be treated with respect.

SOURCE B

Chief Luther Standing Bear belonged to the Lakota Sioux. In 1933, he explained how the Lakota saw the world:

Kinship with all the creatures of the earth, sky and water was a real and active principle. For the animal and bird world there existed a brotherly feeling that kept the Lakota safe among them and so close did some of the Lakota come to their feathered and furred friends that in true brotherhood they spoke a common tongue.

T. C. McLuhan (ed.), *Touch the Earth*, 1971

SOURCE C

In 1911, Brave Buffalo, a Sioux medicine man, described his childhood experiences:

When I was ten years of age I looked at the land and the rivers, the sky above, and the animals around me and could not fail to realise that they were made by some great power. I was so anxious to understand this power that I questioned the trees and the bushes. It seemed as though the flowers were staring at me and I wanted to ask them 'Who made you?'.

T. C. McLuhan (ed.), *Touch the Earth*, 1971

Circles were important symbols. Life and the seasons flowed full circle. The sun, the most powerful of all natural objects, was circular. Thus worship and dances would often take place in circles. Even the tepees were round, and the villages were arranged in circles.

SOURCE D

This painted hide depicts the legend of the snake clan within a circle.

SOURCE E

Black Elk, the Sioux holy man, explained why circles were important:

You have noticed that everything the Indian does is in a circle, and that is because the Power of the World always works in circles, and everything tries to be round. In the old days when we were a strong and happy people, all our power came to us from the sacred hoop of the nation, and so long as the hoop was unbroken, the people flourished. The flowering tree was the living centre of the hoop, and the circle of the four quarters nourished it. The east gave peace and light, the south gave warmth, the west gave rain and the north with its cold and mighty wind gave strength and endurance.

Black Elk, *Black Elk Speaks*, 1932

Spirits

The Plains Indians believed that there were many spirits. These spirits took the form of aspects of the natural world: animals, rocks, rivers, the sun and the moon. Most of the tribes did not believe that there was one supreme being, although the Teton Sioux worshipped Wakan Tanka (the Great God). Many tribes believed that there were three parallel worlds: the earth, the water below, and the sky above. The earth floated on a lake. Spirits below the surface of the lake had power over all living things on the land and in the water. In the sky, a third world existed, where other mighty spirits controlled the sun, wind and rain.

People with special religious powers communicated with the spirits through visions. To acquire these powers, a teenage boy would set off on a 'vision quest', a lonely and potentially dangerous journey. The young man travelled alone to an isolated place. After several days of prayer, fasting and sometimes self-torture, he might see a vision of an animal or bird. He would then have a special relationship with the creature seen in the vision. Often the boy would return to his village in a confused, delirious state. It would then be the duty of the holy man or 'medicine man' to interpret the meaning of the vision.

Native American medicine men had many powers. They organised and led the Native American ceremonies, rituals and forms of worship. By being in touch with the spirits, they made sure that the tribe was in harmony with nature. However, their powers sometimes made them feared and distrusted.

When someone fell ill, the Native Americans often thought that the person was possessed by evil spirits. It was the medicine man's duty to conquer these spirits and make them disappear. This was done with songs, chants, dances and trances. The holy men also had traditional remedies to cure illness. These ranged from ointments

BLACK ELK'S VISION

In his 1932 book *Black Elk Speaks*, Black Elk recalled one of his vision quests. In his dream, he was borne away into the snowy mountains on a cloud. Once there, he saw fantastic visions of differently coloured horses, black, white, sorrel and buckskin, all led by one bay horse. The horses led Black Elk to the Six Grandfathers, the Powers of the World. The Grandfathers took the form of various creatures such as geese, eagles and elk. Black Elk himself became a spotted eagle. He then saw the rest of his people in both human and animal form, and was told that the Six Grandfathers had given him the power to influence his people for the common good. On the top of a high mountain, he saw the 'whole hoop of the world'. The Grandfathers told him that he had triumphed. He now had holy powers in matters of life and death. Black Elk's account of his vision ended with him walking back to his own village. He entered his tepee, and saw his own mother and father bending over a sick boy – himself. He was scared to tell anyone about his experience at first, and it was only when he was much older that he understood the significance of his vision and the responsibilities that went with it.

A medicine man of the Blackfoot tribe, painted by George Catlin in 1832.

and potions to rattles, drums, masks, prayer sticks, magical stones and medicine pipes. For example, the Native Americans thought that tobacco was a highly effective cure for sickness! Each man in the tribe also had his own medicine bundle, in which he kept something sacred to him alone, such as a special plant or a stone.

Dancing

Ceremonial dances were an integral part of the worship of the Plains Indians. The Sun Dance was particularly important. The celebrations lasted for about a week in midsummer, with four days of dancing. As with many other forms of religious ritual, the purpose of the Sun Dance was to protect the tribe. It centred on a pole, around which Native American men (women were not involved) moved rhythmically. No food or drink was taken during the period of the dance. The men of some tribes (the Oglala Sioux in particular) pierced their own bodies, mutilating themselves with skewers or ropes. This was to honour their God, Wakan Tanka.

SOURCE G

A buffalo dance of the Mandan Indians, painted by Karl Bodmer in about 1834.

SOURCE H

In 1915, Chased-By-Bears, a Santee–Yanktonai Sioux, described the Sun Dance:

A man's body is his own, and when he gives his body or his flesh he is giving the only thing which really belongs to him.

T. C. McLuhan (ed.), *Touch the Earth*, 1971

Other dances celebrated aspects of nature that were part of the everyday lives of the Plains Indians. There were bear, buffalo and antelope dances. For the minority of tribes which grew crops, such as the Mandan, there was the corn dance. Ceremonies also accompanied 'rites of passage': birth, puberty, marriage and death.

Unlike the Europeans in the nineteenth century, the Plains Indians did not believe that some people went to heaven or hell. Everyone went to the same place, the Happy Hunting Ground.

>> **Activities**

1 What can you learn from Sources A and G about the beliefs of the Plains Indians?

2 Why was a medicine man an important member of his tribe?

The West in 1840

EARLY EXPLORATIONS AND POLITICAL EXPANSION

> The American West was largely unexplored by white people before 1800, although parts of the South West had been under Spanish influence for nearly 300 years. The region was occupied by many tribes of Native Americans.

> In 1803, the size of the USA had been almost doubled as a result of the Louisiana Purchase. The Lewis and Clark expedition had then set out as the first organised attempt to explore the West.

> Texas had become independent from Mexico in 1836, and it joined the USA in 1845. The later acquisition of Oregon from Great Britain in 1846 and California from Mexico in 1848 gave the US government control of all the land west of the Mississippi.

THE PLAINS INDIANS

> Many Native American peoples lived on the Great Plains. The tribes shared similar lifestyles and beliefs.

> Tribes consisted of bands of 100–500 people. Each band was headed by a chief assisted by a council of elders. In the larger tribes, the chiefs met to take decisions affecting the whole tribe.

> The Native Americans believed that land should not be owned by individuals, and that the earth belonged to everyone equally.

> The Plains Indians were hunters whose existence was dependent on plentiful supplies of buffalo.

> Success in warfare was highly prized by the Native Americans. They had strict codes of honour in battle.

> Men and women, and boys and girls, had strictly defined roles.

> Religious belief centred around the worship of nature and spirits. Medicine men were believed to have great powers.

>> Review question

Was conflict between the white Americans and the Native Americans inevitable?

Fur traders, trappers and mountain men

Some of the first white people to establish themselves in the West were men who worked in the fur trade hunting and trapping beaver in the Rocky Mountains. These trappers were often known as mountain men.

Mountain men helped to open up the West to trade. They spent their winters trapping beaver, living and working in harsh conditions in remote areas.

Fur trapping was tiring, dirty work, but it appealed to men with a strong sense of adventure. They sometimes worked alone, and sometimes with others. The mountain men stood in the rivers of the Rockies to place their traps, with the water reaching up to their waists. They lived in remote camps in conditions that were little different from those of the Native Americans of the region.

The fur traders faced numerous hazards. They sometimes had to eat tree bark or beaver meat because of the lack of food. The climate ranged from the harsh winter blizzards of the northern Rockies to the scorching sun of the southern Rockies. Native Americans sometimes clashed with the mountain men, but in the early years relations were generally good because the Native Americans did not see the fur traders as a threat to their way of life.

In the mountains, grizzly bears were a constant threat. In *Kit Carson's Autobiography*, published in 1858, the famous hunter and trapper Kit Carson described climbing a tree to escape two grizzly bears. 'I got up some ten or fifteen feet, where I had to remain till the bears found it convenient to leave. One remained but a short while, the other stayed for some time… He made several attempts at the tree in which I was perched, but as he could do no damage, he finally concluded to leave. I was heartily pleased at this, never having been so badly scared in my life.'

THREE MOUNTAIN MEN

Jim Bridger

Jim Bridger was born in Richmond, Virginia, in 1804. He was eight when his family moved west to farm near the Mississippi river. In 1822, he joined a party travelling up the Missouri, and he later became a partner in the Rocky Mountain Fur Company. Although he had little formal education, his knowledge of the West and his skills as a guide and scout were legendary. He is said to have been the first white man to have seen the Great Salt Lake. As the West opened up, he began to be in great demand. He worked for the army and acted as a surveyor for the Union Pacific Railroad. He died on his farm in Missouri in 1881, a famous mountain man.

Kit Carson

Kit Carson also began his working life as a fur trapper before achieving greater fame. Like Bridger, he had a thorough understanding of the West. In the 1840s, he acted as guide to the explorer John Fremont. Kit Carson later became a successful soldier, and he was also an Indian agent who represented the US government to Native Americans. He had a reputation for treating Native Americans fairly, and his first two wives were American Indians. He was, perhaps, the first national hero of the West, although he was modest about his many achievements. He died in 1868, aged 58.

James P. Beckwourth

James P. Beckwourth was the first partly black (mulatto) man to become famous in the West. He was born in 1798, and his mother was a slave. For six years, he lived with the Crow Indians. He was known as Morning Star, and he married several Native American women. In addition to working in the fur trade, he was also an army scout, gold miner and guide. He discovered a way through the Sierra Nevada mountains, and this is now known as the Beckwourth Pass.

By the early 1830s, about 1600 men were working for the American Fur Company or the Hudson's Bay Company. The big event of the year in the fur trade was the annual rendezvous. All the mountain men emerged from their camps to meet buyers and suppliers from St Louis at a prearranged spot. Here they would sell their furs and buy their supplies for the coming year. By 1840, however, the day of the fur trapper was coming to an end, and only 120 men met at the rendezvous.

There were two main reasons for the decline in the fur trade:

> Because of changing fashions, people wanted hats made out of silk rather than beaver fur.

> The number of beavers had declined because of the large numbers of trappers.

After the collapse of the fur trade, many of the trappers stayed in the West and became scouts, guides or miners. The real importance of the fur trappers and mountain men had been that they had opened up the West for the huge wave of settlers who followed them.

Discussion points

> If life in the mountains was so hard, why did many white Americans choose to live as mountain men?

> Early travellers in the West used to mistake mountain men for Native Americans. Why do you think this was?

The Oregon Trail

During the 1840s, thousands of people made their way across the Great Plains and the Rockies to a new life in the valleys of Oregon and California. Many of them followed a route known as the Oregon Trail.

What was travelling along the Oregon Trail like?

SOURCE A

Albert Bierstadt's painting The Oregon Trail *(1869). The glow of the sun suggests a future full of promise and success.*

Why people went west

The fur traders had opened up the West, and they were quick to spread stories about the opportunities available out there. Missionaries had settled in the far West, and they also sent back favourable reports about the land and its farming potential.

In those areas in the East that had already been settled by white Americans, land was scarce, and people who wished to farm looked to the West. In 1837, a financial crisis in the East ruined many businesses, and prices for farm produce went down. The people affected by this crisis wanted to farm where land was cheaper.

Other people liked the idea of carrying on the pioneering spirit of men such as Daniel Boone. Oregon societies were formed in some towns to plan migration to the West.

The US government encouraged settlers to go west. Once Oregon and California had become part of the USA, there was a need for Americans to settle the area. The government promised the settlers land.

As the migration continued, the greatest encouragement came from those who had already made the journey. They wrote home to those in the East with inspiring stories.

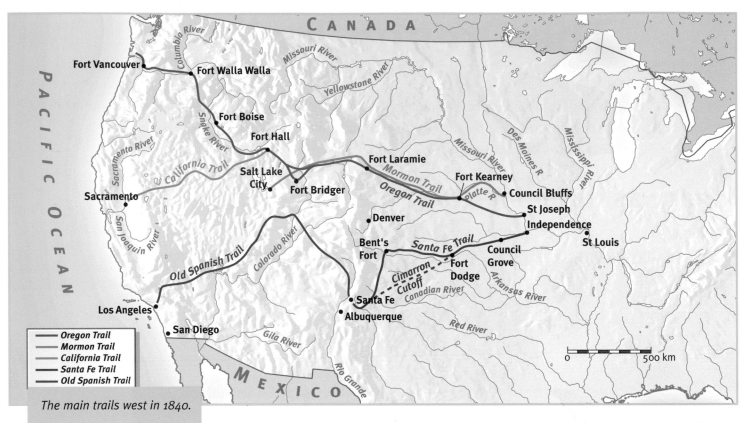

The main trails west in 1840.

SOURCE B

In 1845, Anna Maria King emigrated from Massachusetts with her husband Stephen to the Luckiamute Valley, Oregon. In a letter to her mother, brothers and sisters in 1846, she praised life in the West:

I like the country. I like it well. It is an easy place to make a living. You can raise as many cattle as you please and not cost you a cent, for the grass is green the whole winter and cattle are as fat as if they had been stall fed the whole year round.

K. L. Holmes (ed.), *Covered Wagon Women*, 1983

SOURCE C

Betsey Bayley made the journey to Oregon in 1849. She wrote to her sister:

Oregon is the healthiest country I ever lived in... The climate is mild and pleasant and the air pure and bracing. I have kept fresh meat for three weeks, good and fresh without salt. The country abounds in almost all kinds of vegetation. It is one of the best wheat countries in the world. Vegetables do well... The country produces almost all kinds of fruit.

K. L. Holmes (ed.), *Covered Wagon Women*, 1983

Large-scale migration began in 1843, when 913 people travelled west, mostly to Oregon. By 1848, over 14,000 settlers had followed them. The main starting points were Independence and St Joseph, both in Missouri. These towns were hives of activity as travellers stocked up with supplies and planned their 2000-mile journey.

The Oregon Trail

The first section of the Oregon Trail over the Great Plains followed the Great Platte River Road through Fort Laramie to Independence Rock, a prominent landmark on which it was the custom for migrants to carve their names. After crossing the Rockies at South Pass, the route continued to Fort Hall, where it split into the trails to Oregon and California. Before the settlers could reach their destination, they had to cross more mountains. Travellers to Oregon had to pass through the Blue Mountains with their rivers and rapids, and the California migrants had to cross the Sierra Nevada mountains, which were surrounded by deserts.

To avoid the worst of the winter blizzards in these mountains, people normally began their journey in late April or early May. It was not possible to travel earlier in the year, as there was not enough grass on the Great Plains to feed the livestock. If everything went according to plan, the journey took around four and a half months, with about 15 miles being covered each day.

Transport

Most people travelled in covered wagons, although some pushed their possessions in handcarts. The wagons were light and strong, and ideal for carrying heavy loads over the rugged plains and mountains. However, they had no springs, and were very uncomfortable. A wagon consisted of an undercarriage with wheels. On the undercarriage was a bed for use when travelling and sleeping. A hooped frame over the wagon that was covered with canvas provided protection from rain, wind and snow. The wagons were constructed out of iron and hardwood, such as oak.

Travellers disagreed about which animals were best for pulling the wagons. Oxen were the most popular, but mules and horses were also used. Oxen were slower than horses, but much cheaper. They also adapted much more successfully to the grazing pastures of the Great Plains, because they were less bothered by insects and less prone to disease. Mules were very sturdy, if they could be tamed. Many migrants told of being repeatedly kicked and bitten in unsuccessful attempts to break them. The animals were often involved in accidents, and there was always the threat of a stampede.

SOURCE D

Tabitha Brown emigrated from Missouri to Oregon in 1846, when she was 66. In a letter to her brother and sister in 1854, she described how she kept her spirits up, in spite of the difficulties of the journey:

Through all my sufferings in crossing the Plains, I had not once sought relief by the shedding of tears, nor thought we should not live to reach the settlements.

K. L. Holmes (ed.), *Covered Wagon Women*, 1983

Covered wagons were designed for strength and protection rather than comfort.

Hazards

Many travellers found that they had taken too much baggage. The weight of their supplies damaged the wagons, and sometimes it was impossible to transport the goods all the way. Diaries told of belongings being abandoned along the trail. In M. J. Mattes' book *The Great Platte River Road* (1969), a Dr T, writing in 1849, records that 'bacon, salt, iron nails, boxes, wagon bodies ... clothes, tobacco, trunks ... mattresses, quilts, beef, rice ... handsaws, planes, shoes, soap' and several other items were left behind. Even the wagons themselves were sometimes left if they were damaged beyond repair.

The weather was often bad. It could be very cold at the start of the journey, and a delay could mean that fierce snowstorms would be encountered in the mountains towards the end of the journey. Other problems included violent dust storms, wagons stuck in mud, and plagues of insects such as mosquitoes.

Disease threatened the travellers, and many people failed to survive the long and exhausting journey. Rachel Fisher's story, described in her letters in K. L. Holmes' book *Covered Wagon Women* (1983), was not uncommon. She crossed the Great Plains from Indiana to Oregon in 1847, and lost her husband John and her small daughter Angelina before she eventually reached her destination. Of all the diseases, the biggest killer was cholera.

THE TRAGEDY OF THE DONNER PARTY

In 1846, two families from Illinois decided to emigrate to California. The heads of the families were George Donner, a farmer, and his neighbour James Reed. Their story was to become one of the best-known tragedies in the history of Western emigration, and a horrible warning to future travellers.

The Donner–Reed party made several vital mistakes. It started late, thus running the risk of encountering the winter snows in the Sierra Nevada. The wagons were overloaded: Reed's wagon had built-in beds and it carried large quantities of food and drink. Most dangerously of all, the party followed an untested route, leaving the Oregon Trail at Fort Bridger instead of taking the usual fork at Fort Hall.

The route took the party through the desert of the Great Basin, where morale became poor and tempers flared. In this bad atmosphere, James Reed stabbed to death one of the other emigrants, John Snyder.

It was late October by the time the members of the party started to climb the Sierra Nevada mountains, and they were desperately short of food. It became clear that the snow had made the mountains impassable. They prepared to bed down for the winter in the mountain snow. Starving, they ate glue, toasted fur and dogs. Eventually, they ate their own dead.

Out of 81 travellers, over half died. The rest survived with terrible memories.

SOURCE E

Virginia Reed described her ordeal:

We children slept soundly on our cold bed of snow... Every few moments my mother would have to shake the shawl – our only covering – to keep us from being buried alive.

E. E. Werner, *Pioneer Children on the Journey West,* 1995

SOURCE F

In a letter to her uncles, aunts and cousins in 1847, Mary Murphy told of her plight after surviving all the hardships:

William, Simon, Naomi and myself came through, but as for me, I have nothing to live for ... a poor orphan, motherless, and almost friendless... Now just think of me in a strange country and to think on my poor mother and brother that are dead – their bodies to feed the hungry bears and wolves – for there was no burying them, the snow was so deep.

E. E. Werner, *Pioneer Children on the Journey West,* 1995

SOURCE G

Amelia Knight, who left Iowa for Oregon in 1853 with her husband and seven children, kept a diary:

Made our beds down in the tent in the wet and mud... Cold and cloudy this morning and everybody out of humour. Seneca is half sick. Plutarch has broken his saddle girth. Husband is scolding ... and Almira says she wished she was at home, and I say ditto... We are creeping along slowly ... out of one mud hole and into another. Them that eat the most breakfast eat the most sand... It has been raining all day long...

Chatfield, the rascal fell under the wagon. Somehow he kept from under the wheels. I was never so frightened in all my life. Chatfield quite sick with scarlet fever. A calf took sick and died before breakfast... Here we left, unknowingly our Lucy behind. I was sick all night and not able to get out of the wagon in the morning... Yesterday my eighth child was born.

H. Horn, *The Pioneers*, 1974

In the early days of migration, relations between travellers and Native Americans were generally friendly. Trade was common. The travellers gave Native Americans blankets and luxury items such as beads and mirrors in exchange for food. They also sold them guns and ammunition. While the Native Americans sometimes took horses from the settlers, attacks on wagons were very rare in the 1840s, although it was common for the Plains Indians to demand a payment from the migrants for passing through tribal lands. Confrontations and violence increased sharply in the 1860s when the Native Americans realised the extent of the threat to their existence. However, settlers' wagons were not a major target even then.

There were few facilities on the Oregon Trail. The small number of white settlements (Fort Laramie, Fort Bridger, Fort Hall and Fort Boise) were separated by long stretches of wilderness that took days to cross. The tough conditions meant that arguments often broke out amongst the travellers along the route, sometimes within families.

SOURCE H

Emigrants pause briefly for a rest on the Oregon Trail. Note that the children are barefoot.

Friendship and co-operation

People helped each other more often than they fought. Most wagon trains were well organised, and a captain was usually chosen or elected. There were established routines for each day, and Sundays were set aside for worship. In the evenings, the pioneers often created their own entertainment with music and dancing.

Some people were suited to the outdoor life, and their health improved during the journey. If travellers were lucky and the weather was good, life could often be pleasant. In M. J. Mattes' book *The Great Platte River Road* (1969), one emigrant, Andrew Goodyear, said that he had 'been out 47 days and nights, sleeping with no covering but blankets, and the sky above me for a shelter, living most of the time on buffalo meat – I never enjoyed better health than I do now'.

There were many instances of kindness and helpfulness. Travellers often left messages along the trail to help others following on behind. If a tragedy occurred, people usually looked after each other. *The Great Platte River Road* describes how one pioneer, Margaret Inman, carried someone else's baby for 500 miles after its mother had died. Some artisans and professional people (e.g. blacksmiths, barbers and, above all, doctors) were in great demand, and they helped out the other travellers.

>> Activities

1 If many people, like those in the Donner party, died on the trail, why did so many white Americans still go west?

2 Do you think that bad weather, accidents, disease or inadequate supplies were the greatest problem facing the travellers on the Oregon Trail? Support your answer with reasons and examples.

3 Many of the sources in this investigation are taken from travellers' letters and diaries. Which do you think contain more reliable information for finding out about life on the Oregon Trail: letters or diaries?

The Mormons

A new faith emerged in the USA during the first half of the nineteenth century: the Mormon church. During the early years of their history, the Mormons aroused resentment amongst their neighbours. Eventually, the Mormons moved to the West to escape from persecution.

Who were the Mormons?

Joseph Smith

SOURCE A

Joseph Smith, the first Mormon leader.

The Church of Jesus Christ of the Latter Day Saints (more commonly known as the Mormon church) was founded in 1830 by Joseph Smith. Smith claimed that he had been visited by an angel called Moroni in 1823, when he was 17. Moroni had told him that the true faith was written on golden plates that were buried near Palmyra, close to Lake Ontario.

SOURCE B

Joseph Smith described how he found the plates:

At length the time arrived for obtaining the plates. The heavenly messenger delivered them up to me with this charge: that I should be responsible for them; that if I should let them go carelessly, or through any neglect of mine, I should be cut off; but that if I would use all my endeavours to preserve them, until he, the messenger, should call for them, they should be protected.

J. Smith, *Joseph Smith's Testimony*, 1830

Joseph Smith said that the golden plates told a remarkable story. In 600 BC, God had ordered a group of his faithful believers to leave Israel as Jerusalem was about to be destroyed. They were told to sail to America. Two tribes established themselves in America, one with fair skins and one with darker skins. The tribes were at war for almost 1000 years, and the darker skinned tribe (held to be the Native Americans) eventually defeated the other side. Moroni, who was the sole survivor of the losing tribe, hid the golden plates.

Emma Smith, Joseph's wife, translated the plates. The translation was published as the *Book of Mormon*, Mormon being Moroni's father. Joseph Smith believed that it was his duty to spread the true faith, and he founded a new church: the Church of Jesus Christ of the Latter Day Saints. To the Mormons, the *Book of Mormon* was a sacred text, to be read alongside the Bible.

Smith and the early Mormon settlements

Kirtland, Ohio, became the first Mormon settlement. Initially, the Mormons prospered. They built a large Mormon temple, and many new converts embraced the faith. The strong organisation of the church, which would be such an asset in the future, was already evident.

However, the Mormons were also disliked and feared by their non-Mormon neighbours. In 1832, Joseph Smith was dragged from his bed and tarred and feathered by an angry mob. The troubles of the Mormons deepened in 1837. The collapse of a bank established by Smith in Kirtland caused many of his followers to turn against him. Joseph Smith fled to a small Mormon colony in Missouri.

The Mormons fared little better in Missouri. They were persecuted by hostile gangs who drove them from their homes. To defend themselves, they formed a secret organisation called the Sons of Dan. Violence erupted on both sides. The conflict was close to a mini civil war. Lillburn Boggs, the governor of Missouri, summed up the anti-Mormon mood. He said 'the Mormons must be treated as enemies and must be exterminated or driven from the state, if necessary, for the public peace'. Joseph Smith and his followers were once more forced to move.

SOURCE C

Joseph Smith wrote about the opposition to the Mormons:

Rumour with her thousand tongues was all the time employed in circulating falsehoods about my father's family, and about myself. If I were to relate a thousandth part of them, it would fill up volumes. The persecution, however, became intolerable.

J. Smith, *Joseph Smith's Testimony*, 1830

The Mormons turned back east to Illinois to a small town called Commerce, which they renamed Nauvoo. At first things went well. Illinois was deeply in debt, and the town welcomed the Mormons as a boost to its economy. In return for their votes at the 1840 election, the Mormons were given a high degree of independence. They virtually governed themselves, and even had their own army.

Nauvoo prospered. By 1844, the population had risen to 15,000. A huge and impressive Mormon temple towered over the town. Solid homes were built. Industrial enterprises such as sawmills and quarries were set up. Thriving farms surrounded the town.

However, Joseph Smith overestimated his power and influence in the wider community. In 1844, he angered the non-Mormons by announcing that he was standing for the presidency of the USA. Resentment built up just as it had in Kirtland and Missouri. The first issue of a local newspaper, the *Nauvoo Expositor*, took a stand against Smith and the power of the Mormons. Smith and his brother Hyrum fled to nearby Carthage. Angry crowds followed and broke into the local jail where the two men had sought protection. Joseph and Hyrum Smith were killed by the crowd in the jail on 27 June 1844.

SOURCE D

Carthage Jail, *drawn by Frederick Hawkins Piercy in 1853. Joseph Smith fell from an upper window of the jail and was shot dead as he lay wounded.*

SOURCE E

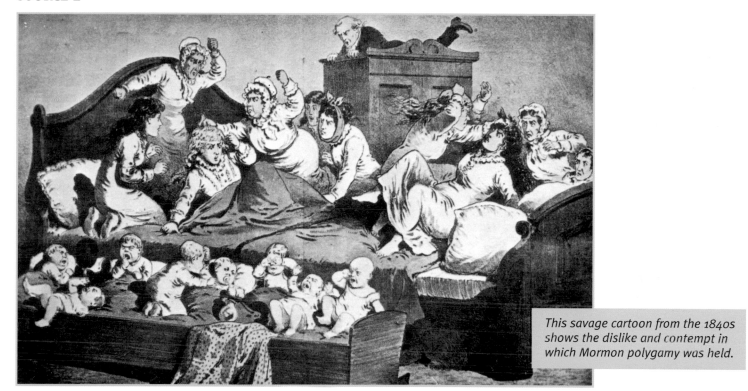

This savage cartoon from the 1840s shows the dislike and contempt in which Mormon polygamy was held.

Mormon beliefs

It was well known that many of the Mormon leaders practised polygamy. Joseph Smith was said to have 60 wives. The first Mormons were opposed to slavery, and many people in Missouri, which was a slave-owning state, were angered by this.

Mormons sacrificed their individual rights in favour of those of the church. Most other Americans believed strongly in individual freedom. The Mormon attitude towards property was also different. Mormon businesses were communal. Everything ultimately belonged to the Mormon church. The fact that these businesses were extremely successful only made people more angry.

The success of the Mormons in converting thousands of people to their faith annoyed non-Mormons. The strength of their beliefs and convictions also made them unpopular. Mormons called non-believers Gentiles. Some non-Mormons felt that they were viewed as second-class citizens by the Mormons.

SOURCE F

Thomas Bullock wrote a letter from the Mormon winter quarters near Omaha, Nebraska, in 1846, before setting out for the West:

The next morning at nine o'clock saw me, my wife, my four children, my sister-in-law Fanny, my blind mother-in-law all shaking with the ague in one house ... when a band of about thirty men, armed with guns, with fixed bayonets, pistols in belt, the captain with sword in his hand... The captain called and demanded that the owner of the two wagons be brought out. I was raised from my bed, led out of doors, supported by my sister-in-law and the rail fence.

I was then asked if those goods were mine. I replied, 'They are.' The captain then stepped out to within four feet of me, pointed his sword at my throat, while four others presented their guns with bayonets within three feet of my body, and said, 'If you are not off from here within twenty minutes my orders are to shoot you... If you will renounce Mormonism you may stay here and we will protect you.'

W. Stegner, *The Gathering of Zion*, 1964

>> Activities

1 What were the Mormons' beliefs?

2 Less than five years after being welcomed in Nauvoo, Joseph Smith was killed by a hostile crowd. Why did people's attitudes towards the Mormons change so quickly?

The decision to go west

After the death of Joseph Smith, it was impossible for the remaining Nauvoo Mormons, now led by a man called Brigham Young, to stay in the town. Young decided to move to a place where the Mormons would be completely free from outside interference. California and Oregon were rejected as they were already filling up with settlers. The area that he chose, a desert region on the shores of the Great Salt Lake at the foot of the Wasatch Mountains in what is now Utah, looked unpromising at first. Nevertheless, it offered three advantages:

> There were no other white settlers there.

> The land could be irrigated, and it was potentially fertile.

> At that time, the region belonged to Mexico, and so it was outside the control of the US government.

SOURCE G

Mormon families pulling handcarts on the journey to Salt Lake City in 1856.

SOURCE H

An 1853 painting of Brigham Young's family by Mormon artist William Warner Major. Compare this with Source E.

BRIGHAM YOUNG

Brigham Young was an effective and inspiring leader. He was a highly organised, practical person. He was fiercely dedicated to the Mormon cause, and he expected others to be as well. Young was a stern man with little sense of humour. After Joseph Smith's death he had complete authority over the Mormons, and he clearly enjoyed this power.

For him, Utah was the promised land, and he allowed nothing to get in the way of this dream. He organised the Mormons with military precision. Each party of travellers was divided into companies headed by carefully chosen leaders.

He realised the importance of raising money, and he sent a Mormon battalion to fight for the USA in the war against Mexico in exchange for funds (and goodwill). In 1849, he established the Perpetual Emigrating Fund. This consisted of cash and livestock granted to potential emigrants from overseas, which had to be paid back when the settlers were established.

Mormons were made confident by their faith and their trust in Brigham Young. They were also brought closer together by their experiences of being persecuted. This encouraged the development of a co-operative spirit. He could be ruthless and violent, but his achievements were considerable. His determination led thousands of Mormons to the Utah desert where they could find peace, prosperity and security at last.

Overcoming the obstacles

The Mormons faced the same hazards and hardships in travelling west as the other groups of migrants: disease, fatigue, bad weather conditions and potentially hostile Native Americans. In addition, the final part of the journey was over largely unknown, dangerous terrain.

The first party of 146 men and women reached the chosen spot in July 1847, and thousands more followed over the next few years. Despite many difficulties and individual tragedies, the Mormon migration went well overall.

SOURCE I

The Mormon William Clayton composed this song in 1846 on his journey to Utah to inspire the Mormon pioneers:

Come, come ye saints
No toil nor labour fear
But with joy wend your way;
Though hard to you
The journey may appear
Grace shall be as your day.

Tis better far for us to strive
Our useless cares from us to drive
Do this, and joy your hearts will swell.
All is well! All is well!

W. Stegner, *The Gathering of Zion*, 1964

SOURCE J

Hosea Stout, one of the Mormon pioneers, wrote about his terrible journey to Utah in 1846 in his diary. Two of his sons died, one of his wives died in childbirth with the baby, and another wife left him:

Often have I lain and contemplated my own sickness and feeble situation without food for myself and family and death staring me in the face. I could only contemplate what would become of them in case I was called away. How often have I beheld my family one by one – yielding up the Ghost, warning me of what may follow. How often in sorrow and anguish, I have said in my heart, 'When shall my trials and tribulations end?'.

H. Stout, *On the Mormon Frontier, The Diary of Hosea Stout 1844–1861*, 1965

The handcart scheme

Brigham Young's judgement was not perfect, and his strong determination to succeed occasionally had disastrous consequences. One such example was his handcart scheme, which began in 1856. The Mormon settlers actually pushed two-wheeled handcarts piled high with their belongings from Iowa to the Salt Lake Valley. Many of the settlers, who were mostly immigrants from Europe, were unprepared for the harsh rigours of such a journey. Two groups started so late in the year that they were caught by early snow in the mountains, and 225 people died before the destination was reached. Many more had to be rescued by relief parties.

A beehive statue outside the State Capitol in Salt Lake City. The symbol of the honey bee was carefully chosen: it stood for hard work and co-operation. Utah is still known as the Beehive State.

Deseret

The Mormons named their new home Deseret, the 'land of the honey bee'. They had succeeded in reaching the Salt Lake Valley because of their confidence, their ability to work hard, and their thorough organisation. These qualities now helped them to build their new community.

SOURCE K

Brigham Young welcomed the first Deseret settlers in 1848 with these words:

No man can ever buy land here, for no one has any land to sell. But every man shall have his land measured out to him, which he must cultivate in order to keep it. Besides there shall be no private ownership of the streams that come out of the canyons, nor the timber that grows on the hills. These belong to the people: all the people.

R. A. Billington and M. Ridge, *Westward Expansion,* 1949

Under Brigham Young's leadership, a co-operative system was devised for irrigating the dry land. While some Mormons worked on the land, others were quick to set up industries, for example in textiles, leather goods, glass and soap making. During the California Gold Rush of 1849, many people passed through Utah on their way to California. The prospectors needed fresh supplies of food and pack animals, which they bought from Mormons. They often needed to sell equipment and machinery before embarking on the last stage of their journey over the desert and the Sierra Nevada.

Creation of Utah

The first Mormons followed Brigham Young to the Salt Lake Valley in 1846/47 to escape from the Gentiles and the US government. They wanted to be independent. At that time, the Salt Lake Valley belonged to Mexico, and the Mormons believed that they would be left alone there to pursue their own way of life. However, as a result of the war which broke out between Mexico and the USA in 1846, the region became part of the USA in 1848.

Brigham Young then decided that Deseret should become a US state, with all the real power being concentrated in the hands of the Mormons. In 1849, he proposed the new state, and was elected its governor by the Mormons. The important government positions were filled by leading members of the church.

The US government resisted this development. It wanted to have as much influence as possible in the newly settled lands of the USA, and it was still very suspicious of the Mormons and alarmed by their custom of polygamy. The government made the region a US territory rather than a US state. This meant that it could appoint the governor and administer the law within the territory. It rejected the name of Deseret, and called the territory Utah, after the local Ute Indians.

The Mormons still had a great deal of freedom in the territory. Brigham Young was appointed the first official governor of Utah in 1850. The other important administrative posts were divided equally between Mormons and Gentiles. At first, there was little interference from the Gentiles in the running of the new territory, but the appointment of three anti-Mormon judges in 1855 changed the situation. In 1857, they returned to Washington DC with exaggerated reports of violence and lawlessness in the territory.

On reaching Deseret, Brigham Young declared 'here we shall build a temple to our God'. The Mormon Temple was completed in 1893, and it stands in the heart of Salt Lake City.

The Mountain Meadows massacre

Because of its concerns about what was happening in Utah in 1857, the US government decided to appoint a new Gentile governor. He was sent out to the territory with 2500 troops for protection. The Mormons thought that the troops were being sent to suppress them, and the tension mounted.

The victims of this ill feeling were 140 men, women and children, who were murdered as they passed through the territory on their way from Missouri to California in what became known as the Mountain Meadows massacre. Most people believed that the Mormons were responsible for the incident, although the Mormon leaders blamed it on Native Americans.

The US government was convinced that a peaceful solution to the problem was needed. A compromise was reached. The governors appointed to Utah were Gentiles, but Brigham Young continued to run the territory in practice until his death in 1877. Polygamy was officially renounced by the Mormons in 1890, and Utah became a state six years later.

>> **Activities**

1 In what ways were the Mormons' journeys to Utah

   a similar to the journeys along the Oregon Trail;

   b different from the journeys along the Oregon Trail?

2 'Brigham Young was more important than Joseph Smith as a leader of the Mormons.' Use the information in this investigation to explain whether you agree or disagree with this view.

Miners and mining

D. Lavender's book *The Great West* (1965) describes how, on 24 January 1848, Henry Bigler made this entry in his diary: 'This day some kind of mettle was found in the tail race that looks like goald. Goald it was.' Bigler was writing about the discovery of gold at Sutter's Mill, California, the first significant find of valuable metal deposits in the West.

What impact did mining have on the development of the West?

1849 saw the California Gold Rush, an event which greatly accelerated the development of the West. Thousands of men (there were relatively few women and children) of many different nationalities flocked to California. This enthusiastic response was repeated when there were further discoveries in other places, such as Colorado and Nevada.

SOURCE A

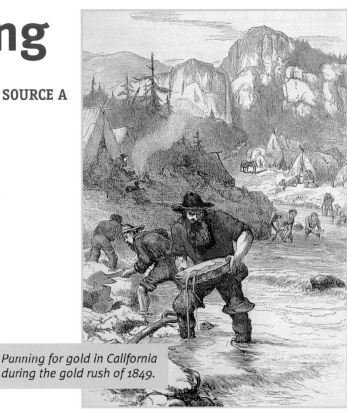

Panning for gold in California during the gold rush of 1849.

The miners were attracted by the possibility of adventure and by the prospect of a better life, and above all by the chance to 'get rich quick' (a favourite slogan of the time).

SOURCE B

A California miners' song captured the exhilarating atmosphere:

Gold out there, and everywhere
And everybody is a millionaire
You'll get rich quick by taking up a pick
And diggin' up a chunk as big as a brick.

W. C. Davis, *The American Frontier,* 1992

PRINCIPAL MINERAL DISCOVERIES 1848–90

Year	Place	Main deposits
1848	Sutter's Mill, California	Gold
1859	Pike's Peak, Colorado	Gold
1859	Virginia City, Nevada (Comstock Lode)	Silver, gold
1860s	Various sites in Montana and Idaho	Gold
1875	Black Hills, South Dakota	Gold
1876	Leadville, Colorado	Silver
1878	Tucson, Arizona	Silver
1878	Tombstone, Arizona	Silver
1882	Butte, Montana	Copper
1890	Cripple Creek, Colorado	Gold

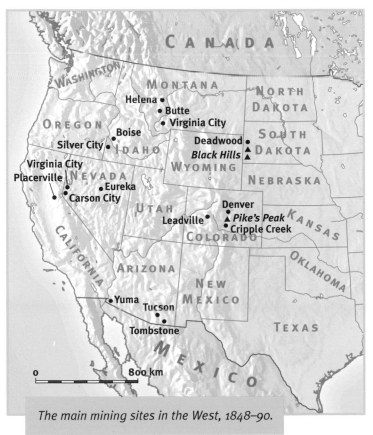

The main mining sites in the West, 1848–90.

The early miners

The first miners were a cross-section of American society, from college graduates to illiterates, from homesick married men who wrote desperate letters to their wives to rootless wanderers, and from slave owners to black Americans. Huge numbers came from outside the USA. In the first wave of migration, about 25,000 men came over from China and thousands more crossed the border from Mexico. There was often racial tension between the white miners and those from other ethnic groups.

The early miners needed neither experience nor sophisticated equipment for 'placer' mining, in which metal ore was extracted from loose deposits such as sand or gravel, often at the edges of rivers. A miner only needed a shovel to tip the gravel or sand into a pan. He then swirled water around in the pan to wash away the sand or gravel and leave the particles of metal. This was called 'panning'. Placer mining was back-breaking work that involved continual bending and standing in cold water. Flooding could easily wash away the potential source of income.

Sometimes two or three miners worked together using more complex equipment, such as a cradle in which the sand or gravel was washed away from the river, or sluices in which the lighter particles were washed away, leaving the heavier particles of metal to sink to the bottom. Some prospectors were successful and did indeed 'get rich quick'. Most toiled away with little reward.

In the absence of an established system of law and order, the miners organised themselves. Access and rights to land were usually divided democratically, with each miner being allotted an equal share in a new area. The miners took the law into their own hands and punished any 'lawbreakers' without waiting for government approval. As there were no jails in the early encampments, punishments could be crude and cruel. Ears might be cut off, and floggings were commonplace. In January 1849, the camp of Dry Diggings became Hangtown, a change of name that tells its own story.

The first miners simply used pans to wash the ore. Cradles were a little more sophisticated, and they were used by two or three men.

SOURCE C

Virginia City, Nevada, where the Comstock Lode was discovered. Like other mining towns, this had a distinctly temporary look.

The mining towns

Most mining settlements were shabby places. Gambling and prostitution were common. Diseases such as cholera thrived. Settlements could be short-lived, and abandoned as quickly as they had been created as soon as the mineral deposits were exhausted. Within a year of the discovery of gold in 1863, Virginia City, Montana, had 4000 inhabitants and a wide array of saloons and gambling houses, not to mention stores and churches. By 1870, the gold was worked out and the town was in decline.

SOURCE D

The author Mark Twain described the conditions in the mining settlements:

But they were rough in those times! They fairly revelled in gold, whiskey, fights and fandangoes, and were unspeakably happy. The honest miner raked from a hundred to a thousand dollars out of his claim a day, and what with the gambling dens and the other entertainments, he hadn't a cent the next morning if he had any sort of luck.

Mark Twain, *Roughing It,* 1872

The rush of people to the mining camps played a major part in the general development of the American West. The miners needed a whole range of services. As a result, mining stimulated other industries, such as logging and food production, and provided jobs for shopkeepers and merchants.

The gold rush encouraged the government and businessmen to improve the transport system. Roads to the West were improved and railroads were eventually established. New towns grew up along the routes taken by the prospectors. Both the seaport of San Francisco and the rail town of Denver owed their rapid growth to the influx of miners.

The gold rush also had some negative consequences. It increased the tension between the new Americans and the Native Americans of the West. Mining took place on Indian territory. The movement of the miners to the West disrupted the lives of many Native Americans as the miners advanced across the Great Plains.

The growth of the mining corporations

It gradually became much more difficult to extract mineral deposits as those near the surface were exhausted. It became necessary to tunnel or quarry into the sides of mountains. Mining became a more complex and costly operation that required shafts, hoists, underground transport and blasting equipment. It was no longer possible for individuals to work the deposits. Large companies and corporations took over. Men who had journeyed to the West in the spirit of adventure and discovery became mere employees. Many mine proprietors were absentee owners who lived back in the comfortable cities of the East.

SOURCE E

In the mid-1860s, the Gold Hill News *reported on work in the Comstock mines:*

The operatives were collected in a large room connected with the engine-room, waiting for the roll-call, which took place at five o'clock, each man answering to his name as the same was called by the time-keeper, and immediately after starting to his place – and as the last name was called, those that had been at work passed out, each one giving his name as he passed which was checked by the time-keeper. By this means no mistake is made, and punctuality is secured which otherwise could not be done.

P. N. Limerick, *The Legacy of Conquest,* 1987

SOURCE F

Miners outside the entrance tunnel of a mine. Compare this photograph with Source A.

Large-scale underground mining meant unpleasant working conditions and frequent accidents. Temperatures could be very high, ventilation tended to be poor, and sanitation was often non-existent. Silicosis, a lung disease caused by inhaling dust, became widespread. Explosives and unsafe machinery killed many men.

The dreadful working conditions, poor pay and long hours led to the industry's first labour strike at the Comstock Lode in 1864. By the 1890s, the Western Federation of Miners had been formed, and there were further strikes in Idaho, Montana and Cripple Creek in Colorado.

SOURCE G

A miner's house in Colorado. Miners came from all backgrounds.

>> Activities

1 Mining was hard and dangerous work.
  Why did so many people become miners in the West?

2 How did the miners deal with problems of law and order?

3 Answer the following questions using the information in the investigation to help you:

  a Is Source B of this investigation a reliable source of evidence about mining in California?

  b Why do you think the photograph in Source F of this investigation was taken?

  c Does Source D of this investigation support Source B? Explain your answer.

  d Do Source E and Source F of this investigation help to explain why there was a strike at the Comstock Lode in 1864?

4 'Mining in the West was badly organised.'
  Do you agree with this view? Use the information and the sources in this investigation to help you with your answer.

The pioneers

FUR TRADERS, TRAPPERS AND MOUNTAIN MEN

> Fur trappers and traders were amongst the first white people to move to the West.

> Fur trapping was tiring and dangerous work. A hostile climate, grizzly bears, poor diet and the threat of unfriendly Native Americans were some of the hazards that the mountain men faced.

> By the 1830s, most of the fur trappers worked for either the American Fur Company or the Hudson's Bay Company.

> By 1840, the day of the fur trapper was coming to an end. The trade declined because fashions changed and beavers became scarce.

THE OREGON TRAIL

> Large-scale migration to Oregon and California began in the 1840s. Most people travelled there along a route known as the Oregon Trail. By 1848, over 14,000 people had used the trail.

> People migrated for many reasons, including favourable reports from the earliest settlers, lack of opportunities and financial problems in the East, and government encouragement.

> The Oregon Trail was 2000 miles long, much of it over difficult terrain. The journey took about four and a half months. Careful planning was essential, and travellers usually started in April so that they would arrive before winter.

> The settlers travelled in covered wagons. Oxen were the most popular choice for hauling the wagons.

> Problems on the trail included overloading of wagons, bad weather, disease, accidents and theft.

> Some people enjoyed the journey, finding the lifestyle healthy. The pioneers were usually friendly and helpful to each other.

MINERS AND MINING

> Thousands of people went west during the 1849 California Gold Rush. They went to 'get rich quick', but few did. The miners came from all classes, races and backgrounds.

> At first, miners could mine metallic ore on their own or in small groups, without needing much equipment.

> The first mining settlements were rough and lawless places. The miners made their own law.

> Mining had a great impact on the West. Industry, transport and towns all expanded as a result of mining.

> As the surface deposits ran out, more complex machines and equipment were needed to extract the ores. Mineral deposits in places such as Colorado and Nevada were buried deep under the ground. Large companies took over the mining industry. Safety standards and working conditions for the miners were often very poor.

THE EARLY HISTORY OF THE MORMONS

> The Mormon church (more correctly known as the Church of Jesus Christ of the Latter Day Saints) was founded in 1830 by Joseph Smith.

> Joseph Smith claimed that he had been visited by the angel Moroni. Moroni told Smith that the true faith had been written on golden plates that had been buried hundreds of years earlier. The writing on the plates was translated and published as the *Book of Mormon*, a book of Mormon scripture.

> The Mormons settled in several places in the East but they were met with hostility from their neighbours. Joseph Smith was murdered in 1844.

> The Mormons were strongly disliked because some of them practised polygamy and they believed in communal rights rather than individual freedom. They had achieved considerable power and independence, and they were very successful in making converts.

> Led by Brigham Young, who was a powerful and determined man, the Mormons departed for what is now Utah, where there were no other white settlers. The first party arrived in 1847, and thousands more Mormons followed.

> The Mormons succeeded in establishing themselves in Deseret because of their strong leadership, good organisation, powerful faith and co-operation.

> After some resistance by the US government to the establishment of a Mormon state, Brigham Young became governor of the new US territory of Utah in 1850. At first, there was little interference from the Gentiles, but tension gradually mounted. This exploded in 1857 with the imposition of a new Gentile governor and the Mountain Meadows massacre.

> A settlement was eventually reached between the Mormons and the US government, and Utah became a US state in 1896.

>> Review question

Why, despite all the hardships, did so many white Americans go west?

Transport and the coming of the railroad

America is a vast continent. The lack of any transport facilities meant that the first settlers spent over four months travelling from the East to the West. Efforts were made to develop better transport systems.

How did people travel across the West?

Settlers in Oregon and California needed regular deliveries of mail and goods from the East. The first miners looked for the fastest possible way to reach California, and the mining industry helped to open up the West. There were several attempts to improve communications across the USA.

Steamboats and shipping

By the 1820s, steamboats were sailing up the Missouri to St Louis and Independence. The fur traders were regular passengers. Conditions on the boats were cramped. People, freight and livestock competed for space. The early steamboats could also be dangerous. They used high-pressure steam engines. If a boiler burst, passengers could be scalded to death.

Later, conditions began to improve. Steamboats became grand and refined. More and more rivers became navigable, and the boats went further into the heart of the West. However, the journey took months, which meant that steamboats had no long-term future.

SOURCE A

A print of a steamboat on the Mississippi in 1855.

Sea travel was another option for those wanting to go west. In the days before the opening of the Panama Canal in 1914, this involved an enormously long trip round Cape Horn into the Pacific Ocean and up to San Francisco. This was not only slow but expensive. The fare by sea from New York to San Francisco was over $500. In 1848, the US government awarded a contract to the United States Steamship Company to carry mail to the West Coast via Panama, where it was taken overland from the Caribbean to the Pacific. This was a very slow and cumbersome way of sending letters.

Stagecoaches

The new settlers soon became dissatisfied with the time it took to send mail back to their friends and relations in the East. In 1856, 75,000 Californians signed a petition calling for an efficient overland mail service.

Two years later, the Butterfield Overland Mail started its first deliveries. This company chose a southern route to California through Arkansas, Texas and Arizona. It was a long route, but the company thought that the climate was more favourable in the south.

SOURCE B

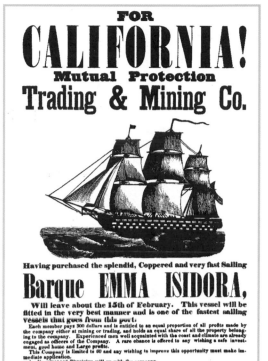

An advertising card from 1849. The discovery of gold saw thousands flock to California. Sea travel was an early, if short-lived, mode of transport.

Concord stagecoaches were used to transport passengers and deliver mail.

The Butterfield stagecoaches carried passengers as well as mail. The journey took 25 days, with passengers stopping at regular stops or 'stages' along the way. The service was reliable but uncomfortable. The stages were rough, with dirt floors and basic furniture. The food was of poor quality, and it included condemned army bacon. The vehicles, called Concord stagecoaches, were more sturdy than previous designs. They were solid enough to cushion travellers from the worst effects of the bumpy roads. The coaches were usually pulled by six horses and staffed by a driver and one or two armed guards.

Although the stagecoach service was a success, the route was abandoned in 1861 because of the American Civil War. It was no longer possible to pass through states such as Arkansas and Texas which had temporarily broken away from the USA. The company accepted a government subsidy to switch to the Central Overland Route.

The Pony Express

In 1860, the young William F. Cody, the legendary Buffalo Bill, rode 322 miles in 21 hours using 21 horses as a rider for the Pony Express. The more typical work of the Pony Express riders was also impressive. A relay of riders carried mail and government documents from Missouri to California in only ten days. Each rider rode 70 miles. As one rider completed his stage, the next was ready to take over immediately. The mail was carried in a pair of saddle bags, and it was transferred with great speed like a baton in a relay race.

The Pony Express lasted for just over a year, but in that short space of time it became one of the most famous and romantic episodes in Western history. It was started by William H. Russell, W. B. Waddell and Alexander Majors, who already operated transport ventures throughout the West. In the mid-1850s, they controlled the freighting industry on the Great Plains with a fleet of wagon trains. They operated stagecoach operations such as the Leavenworth and Pike's Peak Express Company, which served the gold mines in Colorado. Their businesses, though, were losing money. The Pony Express was their last hope of success.

Unfortunately for the partners, the Pony Express did not make a profit. It failed for two main reasons:

> The government refused to give the Pony Express a subsidy to carry mail. Russell was considered untrustworthy, and he later spent time in jail for fraud.

> In October 1861, the telegraph wires from the East and the West were joined at Salt Lake City. Messages from New York could then reach San Francisco in one day.

The Pony Express was short-lived, but spectacular and fondly remembered.

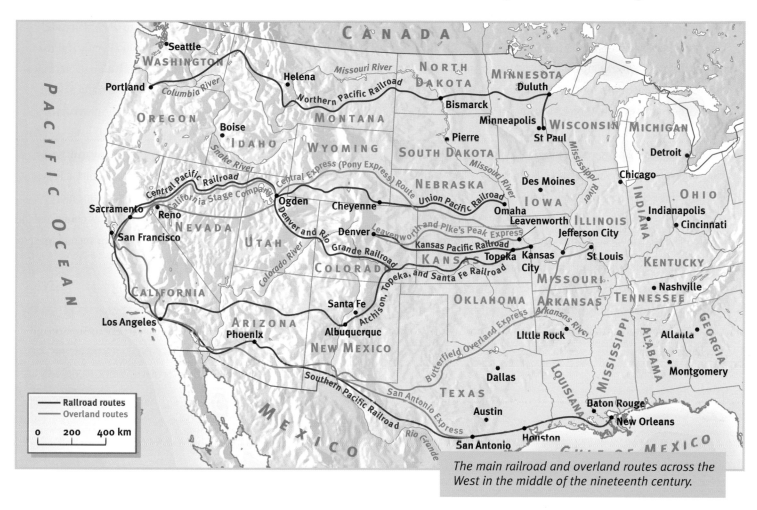

The main railroad and overland routes across the West in the middle of the nineteenth century.

The transcontinental railroad

The defeat of Mexico and the acquisition of California in 1848 gave rise to a sense of nationalism in the USA: one nation stretching from coast to coast. The idea of 'manifest destiny' caught the public imagination. The US government had shown itself to be willing to promote national unity by subsidising shipping and stagecoach lines. The growing numbers of miners and settlers in the West had to be supported. This called for a bigger project altogether: a transcontinental railroad.

The route

There was a lively debate about which route the railroad should take. Some people wanted a central route, and others argued for a southern one following the original Butterfield stage line. To settle the argument, the US government asked the US army to survey all the possible courses west of the Mississippi. This made matters worse, because the survey suggested not two but four possible routes. The debate was ended by the Civil War; all the southern routes were blocked by the breakaway Confederate states. A central route was chosen.

Two companies built the railroad tracks. The Central Pacific Railroad started in Sacramento, California, and worked its way east over the Sierra Nevada. The Union Pacific Railroad struck out west through the Great Plains and the Rockies. The two sets of tracks were supposed to meet at the California–Nevada border.

Funding

Generous financial support was offered to the railroad companies by the government in the form of loans and grants. They received $16,000 for each mile in flat country, $32,000 for each mile in the foothills, and $48,000 for each mile in the mountains. The government also gave the companies strips of land next to the track. This could be sold to settlers to bring in more money.

Despite this support, the Union Pacific Railroad could not raise all the finance it needed at first, and its land grant had to be doubled. As work progressed, the government continued to assist the companies. They classified the plains in Utah as mountain country and allowed the companies the maximum subsidy of $48,000 per mile.

Problems and progress

Both companies had problems. The Central Pacific Railroad workers had to quarry through the Sierra Nevada mountains, constructing many tunnels and bridges. Labour was difficult to obtain. The company's solution was to import vast numbers of Chinese workers. The Chinese were often badly treated, and prejudice against them was common. The Union Pacific Railroad also suffered from a labour shortage. The Civil War lasted until 1865, and this deprived the railroad of an enormous number of potential workers. With the end of the war things improved, and thousands of Irish labourers came west to help build the railroads.

Living conditions for those building the railroad were often squalid. Temporary shanty towns grew up that were similar to the mining camps. Saloons, dance halls, gamblers and prostitutes came and went. The towns were usually abandoned when the railroad moved on.

The two companies raced against each other to see which could build the most miles of track. In 1868, the Union Pacific Railroad built 425 miles of track and the Central Pacific Railroad 360 miles. So great was the enthusiasm that the two crews initially passed each other going in opposite directions! Wisely, the government ordered them to meet up at Promontory Point, in Utah. On 10 May 1869, Leland Stanford, a railroad promoter, got ready to drive a golden spike into the railroad track at Promontory Point. He swung a heavy hammer – and missed! He tried again, this time more successfully. This was the last link in a track that now connected the Atlantic to the Pacific. A railroad crossed the USA from one coast to the other. The whole country celebrated.

Later railroads

From 1870, main rail routes and branch lines sprang up all over the West. Some of the most important were the Atchison, Topeka and Santa Fe Railroad, the Denver and Rio Grande Railroad, the Southern Pacific Railroad, and the Northern Pacific Railroad.

SOURCE C

Chinese coolies working on the Central Pacific Railroad.

SOURCE D

The Golden Spike Ceremony (10 May 1869) at Promontory Point, Utah, where the Central Pacific Railroad met the Union Pacific Railroad.

THE IMPACT OF THE RAILROADS

The railroads brought new problems to the West. Conflicts between the Plains Indians and the white settlers and the US army became more fierce. The Native Americans saw the railroads as a major threat to their way of life.

The coming of the railroads helped the West to develop and grow in a number of ways:

> Cities such as Los Angeles, Dallas and Denver grew large because of the railroads.

> Some of the temporary shanty towns became settled communities, for example Cheyenne and Laramie in Wyoming.

> Thousands of farms were created close to the rail routes. On the Great Plains, the railroads gave a great boost to homesteading farmers.

> Ranching and the cattle industry also benefited from the railroads. Cattle trails ended in cow towns, such as Abilene and Dodge City, from which the animals were transported by rail to Chicago and the East.

> Trade and heavy industry also profited. Raw materials and finished goods could be easily transported back and forth across the country. By the 1890s, the West had become part of the US industrial revolution.

> The West became more civilised and law-abiding, because federal marshals, government officials and teachers could travel in comfort to take up posts in the West.

> Many Chinese people settled in the West, especially in California. By 1870, the Chinese population of California was over 75,000.

>> Activities

1 Draw a timeline for the American West that starts in 1820 and ends in 1870. Mark on the timeline the transport developments outlined in this investigation. Explain which development, in your opinion, was the most significant.

2 Were individuals or the US federal government more important in the development of transport systems in the West? Explain your answer.

3 Draw a spider diagram to show the consequences of the building of the railroads. Were the results all good? Explain your answer.

Homesteading on the Great Plains

Until the late 1850s, few families seriously considered settling on the Great Plains. The area was seen as a desert unsuitable for farming, and as an obstacle to be crossed as quickly as possible on the way to Oregon or California.

How did people settle on the Great Plains?

The new Americans gradually discovered that it was possible to farm on the Great Plains. These pioneering farmers were known as 'homesteaders', after their farms, or 'homesteads'. They moved west to seek a better, more prosperous life.

During the next decade, farms and settlements were established all over Nebraska and Kansas, the states immediately to the west of the Missouri river. From 1868, South Dakota became popular. Even more settlers poured into this area when gold was discovered in the Black Hills in 1875. By 1895, there were more than 430,000 homesteads in Kansas, Nebraska, North Dakota and South Dakota.

By the 1880s, homesteading had pushed far to the west; even the high plains and mountain areas of Wyoming and Montana were attracting farmers. This country was not so suitable for cultivation, and Wyoming is still today one of the most sparsely populated states in the USA.

Why homesteaders moved out to the West

Good farmland was scarce in the East. Competition for land was strong in the Mississippi valley, and this encouraged people to try their luck elsewhere.

Thousands of the homesteaders came from abroad, especially northern Europe. Large numbers of German settlers moved out to the Great Plains. Many Norwegians, Swedes and Danes settled in Minnesota and in the Dakotas. Hundreds of place names in Minnesota today have Scandinavian origins.

At the end of the Civil War in 1865, many veterans wished to make a fresh start in a new part of the country. The war had brought an end to slavery, but former slaves from the defeated South still faced persecution and uncertainty at home. Despite opposition and hostility from some white homesteaders, some black people set out to find a new life in the West. Small black homesteading communities were established, particularly in parts of Kansas.

SOURCE A

Homesteaders outside their sod house in Nebraska in 1886. The pile of antlers in the foreground would be ground down and used for fertiliser.

NICODEMUS

Thomas Johnson was a former slave who lived in Kentucky. In 1877, he was one of 300 people who banded together to leave their town. A leaflet had been circulated encouraging black people to go to Kansas.

Johnson was one of the original founders of Nicodemus, Kansas. The town was named after a proud and respected slave. The settlers had a hard time at first. Crops failed, storms raged, and they had to live in dugouts before proper houses could be built. Nicodemus still exists today – the last black settlement left in Kansas.

The 1862 Homestead Act

The US government played a key part in encouraging the homesteaders. The politicians in Washington DC were keen to see US citizens settling in the new Western territories. In 1862, the government passed the Homestead Act to encourage migration.

The Homestead Act stated that all heads of household and males over the age of 21 could receive 160 acres of land in the Western territories if they built a house on their plot and lived and worked on the land for five years. An entry fee of $10 had to be paid immediately. Alternatively, an individual could pay the government $1.25 an acre and be given the land after six months.

SOURCE B

All Colored People

THAT WANT TO

GO TO KANSAS,

On September 5th, 1877,

Can do so for $5.00

IMMIGRATION.

Whereas, We, the colored people of Lexington, Ky,. knowing that there is an abundance of choice lands now belonging to the Government, have assembled ourselves together for the purpose of locating on said lands. Therefore,

Be it Resolved, That we do now organize ourselves into a Colony, as follows:— Any person wishing to become a member of this Colony can do so by paying the sum of one dollar ($1.00), and this money is to be paid by the first of September, 1877, in instalments of twenty-five cents at a time, or otherwise as may be desired.

Resolved, That this Colony has agreed to consolidate itself with the Nicodemus Towns, Solomon Valley, Graham County, Kansas, and can only do so by entering the vacant lands now in their midst, which costs $5.00.

Resolved, That this Colony shall consist of seven officers—President, Vice-President, Secretary, Treasurer, and three Trustees. President—M. M. Bell; Vice-President—Isaac Talbott; Secretary—W. J. Niles; Treasurer—Daniel Clarke; Trustees—Jerry Lee, William Jones, and Abner Webster

Resolved, That this Colony shall have from one to two hundred militia, more or less, as the case may require, to keep peace and order, and any member failing to pay in his dues, as aforesaid, or failing to comply with the above rules in any particular, will not be recognized or protected by the Colony.

Posters like this were common. This one urged black people to leave the South for Kansas after the Civil War.

SOURCE C

The Act was designed to provide land for anyone who wanted it and could meet the conditions. There is still some debate as to how useful the Homestead Act was. The late nineteenth century saw the biggest growth in farming in US history. Statistics suggest that about one-third of the farms were set up by homesteaders registered under the Act. However, the Act failed many settlers.

The Western Farmer's Home, *a lithograph by Currier and Ives, 1871.*

Problems with the Act

> The $10 entry fee does not seem much today, but at the time it was more than many workers and labourers could raise.

> The amount of land offered was too small. 160 acres might have been enough in the East, where the soil was fertile, but the land was drier and harder to farm in the West.

> Much of the best land was bought up by speculators and the railroad companies. They wanted to make a profit by reselling the land at a high price. Genuine homesteaders were often left with remote pockets of land some distance from railroads and established settlements.

> The speculators sometimes used underhand methods to get control of as much land as possible. They put up shacks instead of proper houses so that they could claim that particular plots were inhabited. Some of these shacks were portable, and some were actually wheeled around from site to site.

Improvements in the law after the 1862 Homestead Act
The problems with the Homestead Act became clear to the US government. They made it easier for farmers to get more land by introducing the 1873 Timber Culture Act. This Act gave homesteaders a further 160 acres if they planted trees on one-quarter of their land. It also helped with the shortage of timber on the Great Plains.

In 1877, the Desert Land Act was passed. For only 25 cents an acre, an individual could register a claim to 640 acres of land in certain dry areas. After three years, he could acquire the land, providing it had been irrigated, for a further payment of $1 per acre. Although some homesteaders were helped by this Act, much of the land covered by the Act was bought up by big ranching companies. Their claims to have irrigated the land were often suspect.

The 1862 Homestead Act did not make every man a landowner. Thousands of would-be farmers ended up disappointed. Nevertheless, the Act still drove people west and caused them to settle. Much of the land bought by the railroad companies and other speculators was eventually sold to individual farmers.

SOURCE D

Temporary shacks were erected by speculators to help them obtain cheap land.

The railroads

The railroad companies played a considerable part in attracting people to the Great Plains. They had been granted large areas of land by the government, and they wanted to sell the land to prospective settlers. They used powerful and persuasive advertisements to attract buyers. Their posters featured rich-looking farms and healthy, contented families. The Platte Valley, for example, which was in reality a dry and dusty area, was described by a Union Pacific agent as 'a flowery meadow of great fertility clothed in nutritious grasses, and watered by numerous streams'.

The coming of the railroad helped the homesteaders in selling their crops. Trains moved produce to market quickly and cheaply. Wheat consumption was high in the USA. There was also a big demand abroad for exported wheat, particularly in Great Britain.

>> Activity

Which was more important in attracting people to become homesteaders: the railroads or the US federal government?

SOURCE E

Railroad companies had plenty of land to sell. This poster from the 1880s suggests that wealth and prosperity were to be found on the Great Plains.

Early difficulties on the Great Plains

The homesteaders faced many problems to begin with. Even building a house was not a simple matter. Timber was scarce on the Great Plains. Even simple log cabins could not be constructed in many places. The most basic short-term solution was the dugout. These dwellings were simply hollowed out of the sides of hills. The opening was filled with a wall of turf.

Better than dugouts, but still far from ideal, were sod houses. Their walls were made from pieces of turf cut into large bricks. The roofs were made out of timber and covered with more sod and grass. Sod houses had many disadvantages. They attracted insects and they were impossible to keep clean; dry earth constantly flaked off the walls and roof. They were also damp, and the floors could easily become muddy. On the other hand, they were warm in winter and cool in summer, and they were fire-resistant. Some families grew surprisingly attached to their sod houses, living in them for many years. Some people even built grand and spacious ones. Most, though, sighed with relief when they were able to build a permanent house out of timber.

Lack of water was another early hardship. Lucky settlers might live near a stream. Others depended on ponds or buffalo wallows. It was not unusual for people to have to carry water for several miles. The only solution to this was to dig a well, which was a back-breaking task. One person had to dig, and another had to haul the earth up in a bucket. Fortunate families struck water at 30 feet. In the higher areas of the Great Plains, the water table could be 200 feet below ground.

There were few trees on the Great Plains and there was no coal, and so lack of fuel was another problem. The settlers solved this by using the same resources as the Plains Indians: chips of dried buffalo dung. Tightly knotted prairie grass and hay could also be burned in specially built stoves.

Centipedes, scorpions and snakes were all unwelcome visitors. Far worse, though, were the grasshoppers. Grasshoppers ate more than the crops and vegetation. They feasted on clothes, curtains, wooden farm implements and much else besides. In 1874, grasshoppers swept all over the Great Plains, causing immense distress.

SOURCE F

Dugouts were the most basic type of housing. This photograph was taken in Nebraska in 1890.

SOURCE G

A teacher and her pupils outside a sod school in Nebraska in 1889. Sod buildings were often damp and insect-ridden.

SOURCE H

One settler, Elizabeth Roe, described the devastation caused by a swarm of grasshoppers:

They came down like great clouds and settled all over the farm... They destroyed our sweet corn in a few hours on the first day, and still they came – the earth was literally covered with them ... before night there was not an ear of corn or green leaf to be seen.

Elizabeth A. Roe, *Recollections of Frontier Life*, 1885

Spring brought rain and the threat of floods. There was burning heat in the summer and the possibility of drought. Prairie fires were an even bigger hazard, destroying crops and endangering life. Raging high winds could cause devastation – this was 'twister' (tornado) country. In the winter, the land was covered with deep snow. The temperature could be as low as −40 °C.

Women on the homesteads

Mollie Dorsey was 18 in 1857 when she arrived in Nebraska City from Indianapolis with her parents and seven brothers and sisters. Her first impressions were not favourable. She thought that the place was cold and bleak. After a night's sleep she began to change her mind. She wrote in her diary: 'O, but didn't we work yesterday! and we are really trying to be cheerful. The day was beautiful and warm.'

SOURCE I

These extracts from Mollie Dorsey Sanford's diary were written during her first few months on the Great Plains:

8 June: I have been on the rampage for three days, exploring the woods, catching fish, and helping in the garden. We all seem content. Even Mother has caught the inspiration and lost her careworn look and, Mother dear, we will try and make you happy yet.

12 June: A week in our new home already. One would suppose time would hang heavily upon our hands, but no. We all work in the garden. I never made garden before, but then, I'm prepared to do anything.

23 June: I am a little homesick tonight. I am thinking of the many dear friends of the past. My life is not what I pictured it a year ago. The rain is falling in torrents, thunder peals and lightnings flash.

27 July: Nothing of interest has transpired. Occasionally we have had to entertain travellers, all men, not one solitary female but Mrs. Hochsetter and Mrs. Allen have we seen, but we hear of a family only a mile below, where there is a married lady and single sister. We will hunt them up at once.

5 October: Father has built an addition to the cabin of a neat little frame room, so now we boast of a parlour, or sitting room, and feel that we are getting along wonderfully well. We appreciate every little improvement.

Mollie Dorsey Sanford, *Mollie – The Journal of Mollie Dorsey Sanford in Nebraska and Colorado Territories 1857–1866*, 1959

Mollie was determined to make a success of her new life. Her combination of hard work and a cheerful outlook was typical of many Great Plains women. Others, though, found the life lonely and monotonous.

Women ran the home on the Great Plains. The house had to be kept clean, which was no mean feat in those conditions. They decorated the house, often papering the walls with pages from magazines or newspapers because nothing else was available. They made the family's clothes, which was a very time-consuming task. Many households had looms and spinning wheels, although later on these were likely to be replaced by sewing machines.

SOURCE J

Plainswomen led hard and busy lives. They had to do whatever work was necessary around the home and farm.

SOURCE K

A white woman in Kansas gathers buffalo dung for fuel. This was a task that had traditionally been performed by Native American women.

Tasks which seem simple today could take hours. It took a whole day to do the family laundry. In the early days, women even had to make their own soap, and running water was a luxury of the future for most families. Cooking and preparing food for the family was another interminable duty. Before the days of stoves, all the cooking was done in the fireplace, where there would be a spit for roasting meat, big iron kettles and pans, and an oven for baking bread.

Women also carried out many farming tasks. They took on tough manual jobs such as collecting buffalo chips and drawing water. Generally it was the men who worked the fields, but when things had to be done quickly women would help out.

One area of land tended by the women was the vegetable garden. They planted root crops such as turnips and carrots and vegetables such as peas and beans at various times of the year. Women also looked after chickens, pigs and sheep, milked the cows, and made butter.

Life on the Great Plains could be isolated as well as exhausting. However, as communities were established, the women played an active part in drawing people together. Neighbours visited each other regularly. Help was given to the sick; doctors were scarce at first. The women assisted at births and comforted the bereaved.

Dances, plays and social evenings were organised by the women. Sewing bees were common. They took a leading part in religion and worship, setting up Sunday schools and organising Bible readings.

>> Activity

Imagine that your family has moved out west to a homestead. Write a letter back to some relations in the East of the USA or in Europe. Describe some of the hardships your family has experienced as homesteaders.

61

Farming improvements

The farmers of the Great Plains, known as 'sodbusters', ploughed the dry virgin soil and planted wheat and corn. They often used farming methods from the East Coast or from Europe that were not suitable for the climatic conditions on the Great Plains. The shortage of timber was also a problem. From the 1870s onwards, a series of inventions and technological developments made their lives easier and their farms more profitable.

Ranching and the cattle industry had spread across the Great Plains. Wandering steers were always likely to trample and ruin crops. This led to much friction between homesteaders and cattlemen. The solution was to fence the farms, but there was little suitable material to hand. Wood was too expensive to transport from the places where it was easily available. Some farmers made hedges out of the prickly Osage tree. The invention of barbed wire by Joseph Glidden in 1874 was crucial to the farming economy. Within a year, it was being produced on a massive scale. However, this solution was not popular with everyone on the Great Plains. Some cattlemen claimed that water supplies were cut off.

Drawing water from a well by hand could not provide enough water for the farms. The driving winds that swept across the Great Plains encouraged farmers to think about using wind pumps. Machines drilled deep wells, and the wind pumps brought the water to the surface. At first, they were too expensive for most ordinary farmers. By the 1890s, however, they could be bought for $25.

Farmers developed new techniques to use and retain the moisture in the soil; this was known as dry farming. The farmer ploughed deeply, which loosened the soil and allowed the water to move up to the surface. A fine layer of dust stopped the water from evaporating. This did not work everywhere, especially in very dry weather.

The cold climate of the northern Plains killed off the soft wheat brought from the East. Turkey red wheat was a harder type of wheat that was introduced by Russian immigrants. A new milling process made the large-scale cultivation of turkey red wheat possible from the early 1880s.

Many other technological advances were made at this time. It was the era of the US industrial revolution. New farm machinery was imported from the East. Ploughs and harrows were improved. More efficient harvesting machines such as reapers and threshers were also invented in the 1870s and 1880s.

For some homesteaders, these farming improvements came too late. They had to mortgage their land to make ends meet. Others sold up, becoming tenants or leaving the farms altogether. Thousands of homesteaders, however, were helped enormously by these improvements and inventions. Gradually the early problems of homesteading were overcome. Acres of the once-feared Great Plains were covered with wheat and corn.

>> Activities

1 What problems were faced by the homesteaders on the Great Plains?

2 If life was so difficult on the Great Plains, why did so few homesteaders give up and leave?

3 Look at Sources C, E, H, I and J in this investigation. Do they provide reliable evidence that the homesteader life was pleasant or harsh?

4 Why do you think many modern Americans greatly admire the spirit of the homesteaders?

The cattle trade

Fortunes were made by traders who bought and sold cattle and shipped them by rail to the great northern US cities. Cowboys drove millions of cattle across the Great Plains. Later, cattle were raised on ranches on the Great Plains. The great boom came to a sudden end in the late 1880s.

What brought about the rise and fall of the cattle trade?

The cattle industry started in the south of Texas. Like horses, cattle were originally introduced to America by the Spanish. Some of these cattle escaped and roamed free. By 1845, when Texas became part of the USA, there were large herds of unclaimed cattle.

The roaming cattle were of the Texas Longhorn breed. They were the result of interbreeding between Criollos, the Spanish cattle of Texas, and other breeds, such as English Longhorns. The result was an animal with some strong points. The Texas Longhorns were thin and stringy, but they were strong. They could be driven long distances over rough country, feeding on the grass along the way. While other breeds were affected by Texas fever, a disease carried by ticks, the Texas Longhorns were immune.

SOURCE B

The Texas Longhorns were hardier than any other breed:

They could walk the roughest ground, cross the widest deserts, climb the highest mountains, swim the widest rivers, fight off the fiercest band of wolves, endure hunger, cold, thirst and punishment, as few beasts of the earth have ever shown themselves capable of enduring.

Frank Dobie, *The Longhorns*, 1941

At first, there was little incentive to catch the Texas cattle and sell them because the local demand for beef in the West was still small. The big cities of the East were too far away. Some attempts were made to drive the cattle to the big cities in order to sell them. Before the Civil War, cattle were driven up the Shawnee Trail to ports on the Mississippi river. These ventures were small-scale though, and they would remain so until the transport problem was resolved.

SOURCE A

Trailing Texas Longhorns in the 1870s *by Tom Lea. These were hardy animals, but thin. Eventually, they were crossed with other breeds to produce better-quality beef.*

The development of the cattle industry

By the end of the Civil War, there were 5 million Texas Longhorns. Some were owned by ranchers, but most of them were unbranded and they could be taken by almost anyone. Some people began to think that fortunes could be made from these cattle.

The USA was going through an industrial revolution. The factory towns of the North East were growing rapidly. There was a large market for beef for the new industrial workers. Another smaller market also existed in the West. There were large numbers of US soldiers in the region who needed feeding. New settlers, such as the miners, were prepared to buy good food.

The railroads were heading west. The Missouri Pacific Railroad had reached Sedalia in Missouri by 1865. Other companies soon extended the line into Kansas. The railroad system was a way of transporting cattle to the hungry cities of the North East.

There was a possibility of huge profits. Cattle could be bought in Texas for $3–4 per head. In the North, the same steers would fetch up to ten times that amount. Some enterprising people decided to round up herds of Texas cattle and drive them north to the railheads, from which they could be transported by train. This was known as the Long Drive.

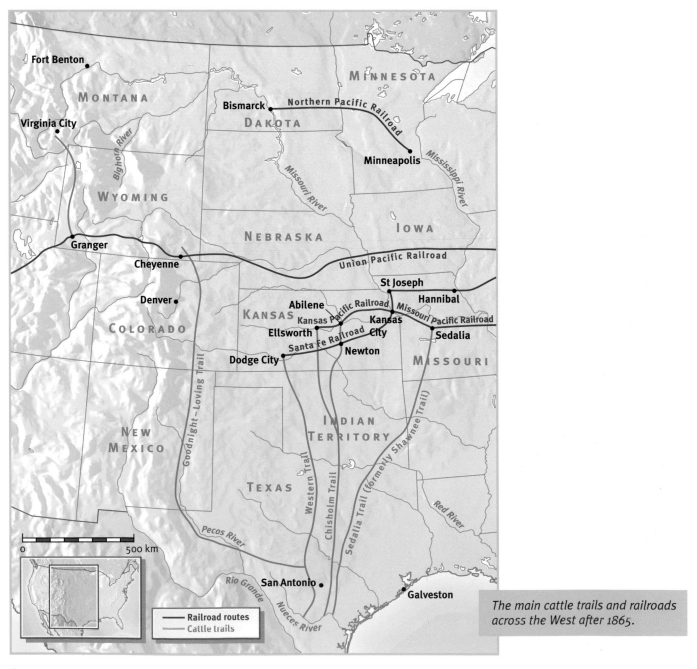

The main cattle trails and railroads across the West after 1865.

DRIVING NORTH: THE EARLY CATTLE TRAILS

The Sedalia Trail

The Sedalia Trail was one of the first cattle trails. In 1866, about 250,000 cattle were driven north from Texas through the Indian Territory (later Oklahoma) to Sedalia in Missouri. It was not a success. Only about 35,000 animals reached their destination. Heavy rains made life difficult for the riders and cattle alike. Some of the route was heavily wooded, and even the Texas Longhorns were frightened of being surrounded by trees. The Native Americans wanted to be paid for allowing the cattle to cross their land. They also deliberately started stampedes, as did armed gangs called Jayhawkers.

The Chisholm Trail

The Chisholm Trail was the most famous of all the cattle trails. It was named after Jesse Chisholm, a half-Cherokee who used the route to trade with Native Americans. The trail went directly north from Texas, across the Red River, and through the Indian Territory, and it ended at Abilene in Kansas. Abilene was a railhead for the Kansas Pacific Railroad.

The success of Abilene and the Chisholm Trail was largely due to an Illinois meat dealer called Joseph G. McCoy. McCoy decided to use Abilene as a place to buy cattle that had completed the Long Drive. The town was on the railroad, but it was mostly unsettled; he could build up the town almost from scratch. Water was plentiful, and the land provided good grazing. Stockyards were constructed, and word was sent to Texas about the advantages of Kansas over Missouri. In 1867, 35,000 cattle arrived at Abilene. A famous party was held, and McCoy and his guests celebrated long and hard. They had much to celebrate. By 1871, 600,000 steers a year were moving up the Chisholm Trail. The railroad shipped them north from Abilene, mainly to Chicago, which established itself as a meat-packing centre.

SOURCE C

Joseph G. McCoy.

SOURCE D

Abilene grew very quickly. This picture is from 1870.

Joseph McCoy eventually went bankrupt, and other cattle towns, such as Ellsworth, Hays and Dodge City, began to compete for the cattle business. However, McCoy's initiative and enterprise had been crucial to the growth of the cattle industry. The traffic on the Chisholm Trail later shifted to the Western Trail. This took Texan cattle to Dodge City, which became the main Kansas cattle centre from 1875.

The Goodnight–Loving Trail

The cattle industry in Colorado owed much to Charles Goodnight and Oliver Loving, who were Texan ranchers. By the end of the Civil War, Goodnight had a herd of about 8000 cattle. With few opportunities for selling beef in Texas, he looked to supply the mining towns around Denver in Colorado. In 1866, the two men drove the herd towards Colorado.

The Goodnight–Loving Trail swung west into New Mexico. Here, by chance, they discovered another market. A Navajo Indian reservation had been established at Bosque Redondo near Fort Sumner. By 1866, the Navajo were starving, and the government was keen to buy Goodnight's beef.

Charles Goodnight.

Goodnight and Loving repeated their drive in 1867, but Loving was killed by Comanches. Goodnight continued to work in Colorado and New Mexico, supplying Texas meat to Indian reservations and army camps.

The cattle towns

Cattle towns such as Abilene and Dodge City grew up almost overnight, and became important commercial centres.

The towns also became notorious as places where the cowboys relaxed, and sometimes went wild, after a gruelling few months on the cattle trails. Law and order was a problem, especially in Dodge City. However, the idea that the cattle towns were packed with prostitutes and criminals is an exaggeration. Even in its heyday, Abilene only had around ten taverns, three brothels and a single dance hall.

SOURCE E

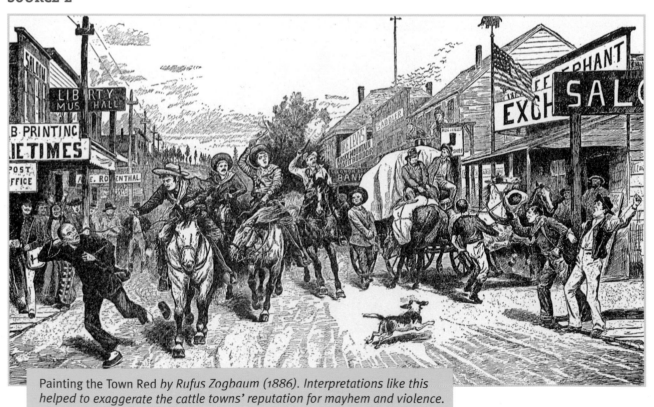

Painting the Town Red *by Rufus Zogbaum (1886). Interpretations like this helped to exaggerate the cattle towns' reputation for mayhem and violence.*

Ranching on the Great Plains

The pioneers of the cattle business drove cattle raised in Texas to market across the Great Plains. During the 1860s and 1870s, many people began to breed and raise cattle on the Great Plains on large farms called ranches. Ranches sprang up all over Kansas, Nebraska and Colorado. By 1868, ranching had spread to Wyoming, and there were ranches in Montana by the 1870s.

The cattle trade on the Great Plains expanded in the 1870s because of new developments:

> The railroad companies continued to extend their networks, and the railroads reached the northern Plains. Cold storage and refrigerator cars appeared on trains. These developments made the transportation of beef cattle even easier.

> Healthier cattle were developed that were better suited to life on the Great Plains. The thin Longhorns were crossbred with other breeds such as Herefords and Angus cattle, which resulted in fatter cattle and meat which was more tender. The new breeds were also better able to resist the cold winters on the Great Plains.

INCREASE IN NUMBERS OF CATTLE ON THE PLAINS BETWEEN 1860 AND 1880

	1860	1880
Kansas	93,455	1,533,133
Nebraska	37,197	1,791,492
Wyoming	None	521,213
Montana	None	428,279

The open range

A Colorado rancher called J. W. Iliff brought large-scale ranching to Wyoming. In 1867, he won a contract to supply beef to the Union Pacific Railroad and its construction crews. He bought $45,000 worth of steers from Charles Goodnight and sold them at a huge profit.

The fortunes made by men like Iliff attracted many more to try their hand at ranching on the Great Plains. Texas Longhorns could still be bought for about $7 a head, and healthy offspring resulting from crossbreeding with Herefords could be sold for eight times that amount.

Land for ranching was cheap; often, it was simply taken. Cattle ranching took place on the open range – acre after acre of unfenced land. If a rancher controlled a stream, he also controlled the adjacent land: usually 30–40 square miles.

This was the heyday of the cowboy, but it did not last long.

SOURCE F

John Wesley Iliff in 1888.

The cattle barons

Much the same thing happened with ranching as had occurred with mining, when within a few years the first independent miners were working for large mining corporations.

In the early 1880s, the cattle business boomed on the Great Plains, especially in Wyoming. Investors competed to plough their money into beef. Thousands of would-be ranchers with no experience of the cattle industry headed west. The inevitable result was overcrowding. Small ranchers were increasingly squeezed out as the large ranching corporations moved in. The cattle barons formed powerful associations to protect their interests.

One typical ranching corporation was the Swan Land and Cattle Company. This was launched by Alexander Swan in 1883. Swan bought three Wyoming ranches, and combined them into a single operation with 100,000 cattle.

The end of the cattle boom

The cattle boom did not last. As more people tried their hand at ranching, cattle became more expensive and beef prices fell because of overproduction. A great deal of money had to be spent on fencing the land. Overstocking of the Great Plains with great herds of cattle reduced the amount of grassland that was available to feed each steer.

Two terrible winters occurred in succession in 1886 and 1887. The second of these caused tragedy all over the northern Plains. Hundreds of thousands of cattle died in blizzards and the intense cold which followed. The temperature plummeted to −44 °C. For much of the time, it was too dangerous for the ranchers to go out, and they were confined to their homes for days at a time. Although many cowboys worked heroically to save as many cattle as possible, the coming of spring revealed the extent of the catastrophe. Ranching continued after 1887, but the cattle boom was over.

SOURCE G

The herds suffered dreadfully in the blizzards of 1887:

Ice-encrusted cattle had staggered into towns and ranches, bawling pitifully. They had knocked down gates, huddled against buildings, pushed in doors, smashed windows in their efforts to find warmth and protection. They had eaten the tar paper off the sides of shacks, devoured the branches, roots and bark of trees. Exhausted, shrunken and starving, they had perished.

L. I. Seidman, *Once in the Saddle*, 1973

>> Activities

1 Divide a circle into four. In each quarter write a reason for the development of the cattle trade. Discuss these with your neighbour. Divide a second circle into six. Write the most important reason at the top, and write the rest in descending order of importance in a clockwise direction.

2 Use your diagram to explain whether the efforts of individuals or impersonal factors such as the demand for beef were more important in the development of the cattle trade.

3 Was the harsh winter of 1886/87 the only reason why the cattle boom ended?

Cowboys: myth and reality

Hollywood images of the West are dominated by cowboys. The movies depict the cowboys as glamorous, exciting people who often resorted to violence.

What was life really like for the cowboys?

Cowboys came to the West from all over the USA. Some were Civil War veterans, and some were labourers from the East looking for any kind of work. Others were black former slaves. Western movies rarely show black cowboys.

The first skilled cowboys were Texans, who had grown used to working with cattle. Many of these were 'vaqueros', cowboys of Spanish–Mexican descent. The impact of the vaqueros on cowboy culture was considerable. Important items of equipment such as the lariat (a cowboy's rope) were first used by vaqueros. One slang word for a cowboy, 'buckaroo', is a corruption of the word 'vaquero'.

SOURCE A

Cowboys on a cattle drive in the 1880s awakening the relief watch to guard the cattle.

COWBOY DRESS AND EQUIPMENT

Cowboys had a hard life. Their work was physically tiring, and it called for practical skills. Their dress and equipment reflected this. Their clothes and tools were functional, and not merely for show.

Typical cowboy dress

> All cowboys wore high-heeled leather boots and spurs. Spurs varied in design, and some had more points than others. Although spurs may seem cruel today, they were often used to make the horses start quickly in emergencies.

> A cowboy's leggings were called chaps (pronounced 'shaps'). They were usually made out of leather, and they were worn over woollen trousers for protection. A cowboy could easily be thrown from his horse, bitten, or pushed against a fence. Chaps also kept out the cold. On the northern Plains, where the weather was cold, they were sometimes made out of wool such as angora.

> Neckerchiefs (also called bandanas) were decorative and came in many colours. Cowboys pulled them over their mouths and sometimes eyes as a shield against dust.

> Leather gloves and wrist cuffs were essential when handling ropes.

> The cowboys' hats were usually Stetsons. These were originally made by a firm called J. B. Stetson, but the name came to mean any similar type of hat. The wide brims protected the cowboy from the extremes of hot sun and driving rain. Ten-gallon hats were less practical and less popular.

Typical cowboy equipment

> Saddles were the most important item of a cowboy's equipment. While cowboys rarely owned their own horse, they always owned their saddles. These usually cost over $30. This was a lot of money for people whose wages were not high, and the saddle would be chosen with great care. Saddles came in numerous designs with many decorated features. One of the most important was the horn, or pommel. The cowboy used this when roping steers. He also used it as a grip when riding at high speed.

> A lariat, or lasso, was used for catching and roping animals. Lariats were made out of horsehair, hemp or rawhide.

> Cowboys carried tools for branding cattle and caring for horses' hooves.

> They also needed a few ordinary possessions, such as a tin plate and cutlery, and a blanket roll.

The Long Drive

The movement of the cattle north along the cattle trails was known as the Long Drive. A successful drive depended on good organisation and routine. Cowboys rose at dawn. After a hurried breakfast, they prepared to strike camp. The herd walked until the hottest hours of the day, when the cattle were watered and grazed. As the heat subsided, the cattle were again driven along the trail. At sunset, the cowboys made camp. The main meal of the day was eaten, and the herd was bedded down for the night. The men took night duty in turns, generally in two-hour shifts.

SOURCE B

Andy Adams rode north from Texas with the cattle drives in the 1880s:

The third animal we struck in the river that morning was the black steer that had showed fight the day before. Knowing his temper would not be improved by soaking in the quicksand overnight, we changed our tactics. While we were tying up the steer's tail and legs, McCann secreted his team at a distance. Then he took a lariat, lashed the tongue of the wagon to a cottonwood tree and, jacking up a hind wheel, used it as a windlass. When all was ready we manned the windlass and drew him ashore.

Andy Adams, *The Log of a Cowboy*, 1903

THE DRIVE FORMATION

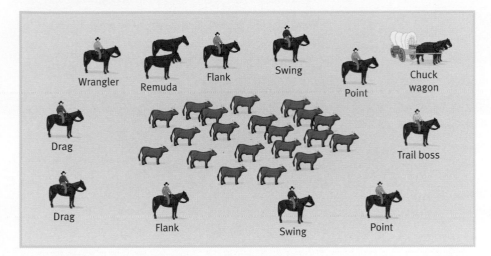

The herds moved along the trails in a set formation:

> The trail boss led the way ahead of the herd. He surveyed the route and looked ahead for the best places to stop and water the cattle. He also tried to spot any signs of danger.

> Alongside him was the chuck wagon and the cook. The chuck wagon was a kitchen on wheels, and it carried all the supplies needed for the journey.

> The point riders were usually the most experienced cowboys. Their job was to keep the herd moving in the right direction.

> Behind them, well to the side of the herd, came the swing riders and flank riders. They made sure that the animals stayed together.

> Last came the drag riders. On every trail, the cattle sorted themselves out, usually staying in the same part of the formation every day. The weakest came last, and it was the drag riders' duty to hurry them along. These cowboys were inevitably left looking after the obstinate, the sick and the lame.

> A supply of horses was also taken along, and this was known as the 'remuda'. The remuda was in the care of the wrangler, who was often a beginner learning the trade.

The size of the herds varied between 1000 and 3000 head. The number of cowboys needed also varied, usually between 8 and 18.

Hazards on the trails

Such long journeys through isolated areas were bound to involve danger. Some hazards, such as Indian attacks and adverse weather, were experienced by all travellers on the Great Plains. Others were a direct result of driving large herds.

Stampedes were particularly dreaded. Minor incidents such as the striking of a match could start the cattle off. A very common cause of stampedes was thunder and lightning. Terrified cattle could head off at high speed in any direction. They could be lost, so badly hurt that they had to be shot, or killed. Cowboys also risked being trampled or crushed to death.

River crossings also claimed lives. Most rivers had to be forded, and some were very wide crossings, such as that over the Red River. Some rivers were fast-flowing and prone to flooding. With hundreds of cattle close together, panic could soon set in. If the cattle at the head of the herd became alarmed, they sometimes caused accidents by turning back into the path of those following. Drought and dust also caused severe problems.

SOURCE C

The Stampede, *by Robert Lindneux, shows cowboys trying to control thunder-frightened cattle.*

In addition to the natural hazards, cowboys also came into conflict with other groups of people. Relations with Native Americans were mixed. Some helped the cowboys, but others started stampedes, attacked lone riders looking for strays, or tried to steal the stock. White rustlers and robbers were more of a problem. They wanted to rob the trail boss of the gold to be paid to the cowboys after the drive north. There was also sometimes violent conflict with homesteaders, who bitterly resented the damage done to their land by the cattle herds.

Far from being glamorous or romantic, much of the cowboys' work was simply dull. It could take up to four months to reach Abilene from Texas. The men became weary, and the long days merged into each other. Stuck with each other's company in a hostile environment, the cowboys often became tense and bad-tempered, yet there was also fun and comradeship. A good storyteller commanded attention and was someone to be admired. Andy Adams wrote that the camp-fire was to outdoor life what the evening fireside was to domestic life.

SOURCE D

These cowboy songs were first sung in 1860–79:

Oh, when I die, take my saddle from the wall,
Put it on my pony, and lead him from his stall.
Tie my bones to his back, turn our faces to the west
And we'll ride the prairie that we love the best.

From 'I Ride an Old Paint'

A cowboy's life is a wearisome thing
It's rope and brand and ride and sing
We ride the range from sun to sun
For a cowboy's work, Lord, is never done.

We're alone Doney Gal, in the rain and the hail
Drivin' them dogies on down the trail.

From 'Rain or Shine'

L. I. Seidman, *Once in the Saddle,* 1973

SOURCE E

The Fall of the Cowboy *(1895) by Frederic Remington. Cowboys worked in all weathers; the winter of 1887 was especially fierce.*

Cowboys on the range

As cattle ranching spread in the 1860s and 1870s, some cowboys became more settled. They spent much of their time working on one ranch. The work here was as tough and unglamorous as it was on the trails. The cowboy was a hired hand performing routine tasks. There were the usual extremes of Great Plains weather, from blazing sun to awful blizzards. Food was of poor quality. The cowboy often lived in a simple shack or dugout. The pay was very low. In 1883, cowboys in Texas went on strike for higher wages.

During the days of the open range, before the land was fenced, the cattle strayed on to other ranchers' lands. Twice a year, in the spring and autumn, cowboys from all over an area organised a roundup. Cattle were identified by their distinctive brand marks, and the herds were separated. Newly born calves were branded. Cowboys on a roundup could spend up to 20 hours a day in the saddle.

SOURCE F

Cowboy Camp during Roundup, *painted by Charles M. Russell in about 1887. Roundups were an important part of ranch life.*

>> Activities

1 How were the cowboy's clothing and equipment suited to his job?

2 What problems did cowboys have on cattle drives?

3 Did the lives of the cowboys improve or get worse when they became ranch hands and no longer rode the trails?

Growth and development on the Great Plains

THE HOMESTEADERS

> From the 1860s onwards, people began to settle on the Great Plains in large numbers. Some went because good farmland was scarce in the East, and others to make a new start after the Civil War. The 1862 Homestead Act, the 1873 Timber Culture Act and the 1877 Desert Land Act offered incentives to settlers. The railroad companies also attracted many settlers with their enticing advertisements.

> In their early years on the Great Plains, many families lived in dugouts or sod houses because there was little timber for building homes. Buffalo chips were usually the only fuel.

> Water was scarce on the Great Plains, and the settlers had to dig wells. Farming was tough going, because the soil was not very fertile or productive. There were extreme variations in climate. Insects could be a serious problem.

> The women on the Great Plains had to look after the children, clean and decorate the home, make clothes, cook, do the washing, grow vegetables, tend the smaller animals, and help with farming tasks. They also played a big part in bringing people together in the new settlements.

> From the 1870s onwards, there were a number of farming improvements. Barbed wire stopped crops being damaged by stray cattle. Wind pumps slowly replaced wells. Dry farming techniques were used. New crop varieties and new farm machinery were introduced.

TRANSPORT

> From the 1820s onwards, steamboats were used by those travelling west. Ships also sailed west via Cape Horn or via an overland crossing through Panama.

> Stagecoach lines such as the Butterfield Overland Mail were successful, but the Pony Express only lasted a year.

> A coast-to-coast railroad was then built by the Central Pacific Railroad and the Union Pacific Railroad with the aid of generous government grants and loans. The companies acquired large amounts of land which they sold at a considerable profit. Labour shortages were overcome with immigrants.

> Other rail lines followed all over the West. New cities and towns were built along the railroads. They brought industry and workers to provide services in the new urban centres. The railroads also benefited farming and ranching. However, the railroads were one of the main causes of conflict between the settlers and the Plains Indians.

COWBOYS

> Cowboys first came from Texas, and later from every part of the USA. They included black veterans of the Civil War.

> They mostly led a hard, unrewarding life, with low wages and poor food, and they had to face many hazards.

> Cowboys settled into a routine on the drives along the cattle trails. The herd moved in a set formation, and each cowboy had a particular job to do. Risks included stampedes, river crossings, dust storms, Native Americans, outlaws and angry settlers.

> Later, cowboys worked on ranches. They organised autumn and spring roundups during which herds were separated and calves branded.

THE CATTLE INDUSTRY

> The cattle industry started in Texas. After the Civil War, new markets, the railroad, a low buying price and a high selling price all favoured cattle owners. Cattle were driven up the cattle trails to the new cattle towns. From there, they were transported to market on the new railroads.

> During the 1860s and 1870s, people began to ranch cattle on the Great Plains, in Kansas, Nebraska, Colorado, Wyoming and Montana. More railroads, refrigeration, and the development of hardier breeds all helped the industry to grow. This was the era of the open range.

> By the 1880s, the cattle business was booming. Large corporations and cattle barons moved in.

> Decline soon set in. There were too many cattle, and they became dearer to buy and less profitable to sell. Fencing costs were high. A dreadful winter in 1887 killed much of the stock.

>> Review questions

1 What problems did white Americans face when exploiting the resources of the Great Plains?

2 How did they overcome these problems?

3 Was life easy after this for white Americans on the Great Plains?

The outbreak of fighting on the Great Plains

The conflict between Native Americans and whites was of long standing. After centuries of misunderstanding and white racism, the Native Americans of the Great Plains went to war against the US army in the 1860s.

Why did the Native Americans go to war?

The Native Americans and the Great Plains

As the new American nation of the USA looked west, the Native Americans seemed to pose a major problem. How could the USA expand when vast tracts of land belonged to the Native Americans? The Native Americans saw the situation very differently. It was their land – the land which sustained them, the land which they worshipped. The two viewpoints were completely at odds with each other.

In 1825, the US government had set up the Indian Territory in present-day Oklahoma, and in 1832, thinking the Great Plains to be of little value, it had granted the whole of the region to the Native American tribes. The Great Plains became one big reservation where, in theory, the Native Americans could come and go as they pleased.

Many Native American tribes were driven onto the Great Plains at this time. The so-called Five Civilised Tribes (the Cherokee, Creek, Choctaw, Chickasaw and Seminole) were forced to abandon their fertile, wooded land east of the Mississippi in favour of a semi-desert region in the Indian Territory that they did not want. In 1839, the Cherokee were forcibly moved west. The tribe was brutally driven on by the US army. Many died along the route, which became known as the Trail of Tears.

On the face of it, the Native Americans looked secure on the Great Plains. Settlers were bound for Oregon and California. The last place they wanted to live was the Great Plains. For their part, the Plains Indians were wary of the migrants, but as long as they were only passing through the Indian lands, an uneasy truce existed.

In the middle of the nineteenth century, however, the situation changed, as soon as white settlers wanted to move onto the Great Plains. This eventually led to war between the two sides.

SOURCE A

The Last of Their Race, *painted by John Mix Stanley in 1857. Why do you think the artist has chosen to set the scene at sunset?*

ATTITUDES TO THE LAND

The two sides had completely different attitudes towards land. For the Plains Indians, the land had a spiritual dimension. Earth, water and sky framed their whole existence.

SOURCE B

Chief Luther Standing Bear described the Native American picture of the world:

We did not think of the great open plains, the beautiful rolling hills, and winding streams with tangled growth as 'wild'. Only to the white man was nature a 'wilderness' and only to him was the land 'infested' with 'wild' animals and 'savage' people. To us it was tame. Earth was bountiful and we were surrounded by the blessings of the Great Mystery.

T. C. McLuhan (ed.), *Touch the Earth*, 1971

To white people, the Great Plains were a wilderness waiting to be tamed, a resource to be exploited, and a potential source of profit. If the land was farmed it yielded crops. If it was mined it yielded minerals. If metal tracks were laid across the land, improved communications helped to develop the economy. They were not concerned about damage to the environment caused by farming, mining, industry and house building.

Native Americans did little farming and mining, and the whites saw this as evidence that the Native Americans did not deserve to control the Great Plains.

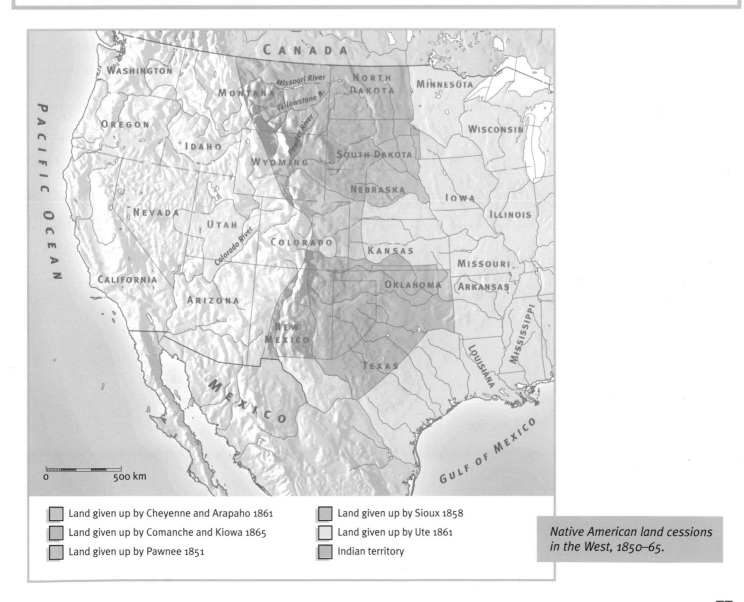

Land given up by Cheyenne and Arapaho 1861

Land given up by Comanche and Kiowa 1865

Land given up by Pawnee 1851

Land given up by Sioux 1858

Land given up by Ute 1861

Indian territory

Native American land cessions in the West, 1850–65.

The 1851 Fort Laramie Treaty

The 1832 agreement that gave the Great Plains to the Native Americans was the first of several guarantees of Native American rights. However, when settlers, mining companies or railroad companies demanded access to new land, such promises were conveniently forgotten. Time and again the Native Americans felt that they had been cheated and betrayed.

SOURCE C

The Native American chief Sitting Bull spoke bitterly about the behaviour of the whites:

What treaty that the whites have kept has the red man broken? Not one. What treaty that the white man ever made with us have they kept? Not one.

W. F. Johnson, *Life of Sitting Bull and History of the Indian War,* 1891

SOURCE D

Some Americans believed that the Native Americans were being treated unjustly:

The attempt to cajole and bamboozle the Indians as if they were deficient in intelligence ought to be abandoned. Faithlessness on our part in the matter of treaties, and gross swindling of the Indians are at the bottom of all this Indian trouble.

New York Times, 8 June 1870

As miners and other white people came into conflict with the Plains Indians, the US government was pressurised to abandon its policy of 'one big reservation'. Some wagon trains were attacked as they travelled on the Oregon Trail, and there was a feeling that the Plains Indians could not be allowed to get in the way of westward expansion.

The result was the 1851 Fort Laramie Treaty. Chiefs of the main Great Plains tribes met at Fort Laramie with Thomas Fitzpatrick, a US government agent. The chiefs agreed to give up their unlimited access to the Great Plains in return for gifts and an annual payment of $50,000 over the next ten years. The main routes through Kansas and Nebraska were to be left clear for the settlers. Each tribe was to be given its own reservation.

This agreement divided the tribes, separating them on their own pockets of land. This made it more difficult for them to band together, and their movements could be more easily controlled.

SOURCE E

Attack on the Emigrant Train *by Charles Wimar (1828–63). Native Americans attacked wagon trains, worried that their land was being invaded by settlers.*

Deteriorating relations

The attitude of the US army contributed to the tension between Native Americans and whites. Most of the senior officers, including General George Armstrong Custer and Colonel John M. Chivington, were extremely prejudiced against Native Americans.

SOURCE F

General Custer saw the Native Americans as savages:

The Indian is a savage in every sense of the word; not worse, perhaps than his white brother would be similarly born and bred, but one whose cruel and ferocious nature far exceeds that of any wild beast of the desert.

George Armstrong Custer, *My Life on the Plains,* 1874

SOURCE G

Colonel Chivington believed that only extreme measures were effective against the Native Americans, and in 1864 he wrote that the Cheyenne must be forcibly subdued:

The Cheyennes will have to be soundly whipped before they will be quiet. If any of them are caught in your vicinity, kill them, as that is the only way.

A. M. Josephy, *500 Nations,* 1995

The hostility of the US army towards the Native Americans was partly based on its misunderstanding of their fighting methods. The Plains Indians placed a strong emphasis on personal courage in war. Displays of individual bravery and the theft of horses seemed to the white soldiers to be evidence of indiscipline. What the Native Americans thought of as courage was seen by their opponents as bloodthirstiness and barbarism. On the other hand, the Native Americans thought that the US army's reliance on fighting together as a unit was cowardly.

Within the US government, the Indian Office and the Department of War both had responsibility for relations with the Native Americans, but their policies differed. Although the officials at the Indian Office had little respect for tribal cultures, they preferred to try and win the Native Americans over to the white American way of life by talking, rather than fighting. However, as relations grew worse, the Department of War became more powerful, and it was keen to use force and punishment to achieve its ends.

The US government policy of confining the Plains Indians to reservations was greatly resented by the Native Americans. They were nomadic hunters who liked to roam the land at will. On the reservations, they were told to grow crops, often on land that was unsuitable for farming. The government officials encouraged Native Americans to abandon their beliefs and language in favour of Christianity and an education in the American way of life. The agents who ran the reservations were frequently corrupt and incompetent. Food was often in short supply, and it could be of very poor quality.

THE EXTERMINATION OF THE BUFFALO

The Plains Indians relied on the buffalo for their survival. When whites settled on the Great Plains, the buffalo herds dwindled dramatically. By 1870, buffalo were rare in some areas. Although there were still around 15 million in total, their numbers had declined by three-quarters since the start of the century. Over the next five years, there was a staggering decrease. By 1875, fewer than 1 million buffalo were left on the Great Plains.

In 1871, it was discovered that commercial leather could be made out of buffalo hides. Buffalo leather soon became fashionable in the East, and there was a huge demand for it. Buffalo hunters flocked to the Great Plains. Pot-shots were taken at the buffalo from train windows. The defenceless creatures were chased across the Great Plains, and their carcasses remained to litter the landscape. Unlike the Native Americans, who used the whole of the buffalo, the hunters were only interested in the hides, and to a lesser extent the tongues.

The US government realised the significance of this. They knew that if the buffalo was wiped out, the Plains Indians would have no alternative but to accept life on the reservation. The killing became more professionally organised. Companies sent out trained groups of hunters instead of relying on adventurous individuals. By 1883, the buffalo had almost vanished from the Great Plains.

SOURCE H

Buffalo hides piled up at Dodge City. This photograph shows the scale of the slaughter and the extent to which the Plains Indians were deprived of their most vital resource.

SOURCE I

The US army general Philip Sheridan was quite clear about the impact of the slaughter:

For the sake of a lasting peace, let them kill, skin and sell until the buffaloes are exterminated.

A. M. Josephy, *500 Nations*, 1995

>> Activities

1 Why did white Americans want to move the Native Americans off the Great Plains?

2 Which was more important in bringing this about: the treaties, or the slaughter of the buffalo? Explain your answer.

3 What can you learn from the sources in this investigation about the attitudes of white Americans towards Native Americans in the nineteenth century?

4 The Native Americans respected all living things. Why, then, did they fight and kill white Americans?

On the warpath

The whites took over more and more of the Indian homelands in the West as soon as they saw a use for the land. They broke the terms of almost every agreement that they reached with the Native Americans. The tensions between the Native Americans and the whites on the Great Plains finally exploded into war in the 1860s.

What happened when the Native Americans resisted white expansion?

The Grattan incident

In 1854, a skinny cow lagging behind a wagon train was shot and killed by Native Americans as it passed by a Brule Sioux village. The cow's owner complained at nearby Fort Laramie. A young lieutenant of the US army, John L. Grattan, led 30 soldiers to the village. After a futile discussion with the village chief, Conquering Bear, the troops opened fire. Conquering Bear was killed. The entire US army unit was wiped out by the Sioux in retaliation.

In the following year, the US army responded by massacring 86 inhabitants of a Sioux village in Nebraska. This made a big impression on a future leader of the Sioux people called Crazy Horse.

The Grattan incident demonstrated how small events could lead on to bigger tragedies and a spiral of revenge and retaliation.

Little Crow's war

The Santee Sioux were a woodland tribe from Minnesota. During the 1850s, 150,000 white migrants, many from Germany and Scandinavia, had settled in Minnesota. Faced with demands for their land, the Santee Sioux agreed to give most of it up in return for agreed annual payments to the tribe. They were confined to a small reservation by the Minnesota River. By 1862, serious trouble was looming. The Santee were in danger of starving: crop yields had been poor, and there was little wild game on the reservation.

The Santee knew that there was food at the US government agency. Government officials said that the Native Americans would have to wait for food until their annual payments arrived from Washington DC. Dee Brown's book *Bury My Heart at Wounded Knee* (1970)

quotes one local white man, Andrew Myrick, as saying: 'If they are hungry let them eat grass or their own dung.'

When the money did arrive, it did not go directly to the Santee but to the government agents. The agents decided to pay off traders who claimed they were owed money by the Native Americans before giving the remainder of the money to the Santee. This was the last straw. In August 1862, four young Native American men were returning from a hunting trip that had been completely unsuccessful. One of the young men dared another to kill a white man. The situation quickly got out of hand, and five white settlers (three men and two women) were murdered.

Little Crow, the Santee war chief, strongly disapproved of the attack, but he was as angry as the rest of the tribe about the way they had been treated. He realised that no member of the Santee Sioux would be safe after what had happened. He decided to strike first and declare war on the whites. The fighting that followed was bloody and fierce. Within a week, an estimated 800 settlers were dead.

Henry Sibley, a former fur trader, was chosen to lead the counterattack against Little Crow and his warriors. He had over 1600 troops at his disposal. Sibley defeated Little Crow's men at Wood Lake. The Santee Sioux surrendered.

Sibley sentenced 306 of the Santee Sioux to death. Each of the so-called trials leading to the sentences lasted about 5 minutes, and little real evidence was heard. The US President, Abraham Lincoln, intervened. While he could not agree with the violence and murder that had taken place, he realised that the Santee had been badly treated. The number of those condemned to be hanged was reduced to 38. It was still the largest mass execution in US history.

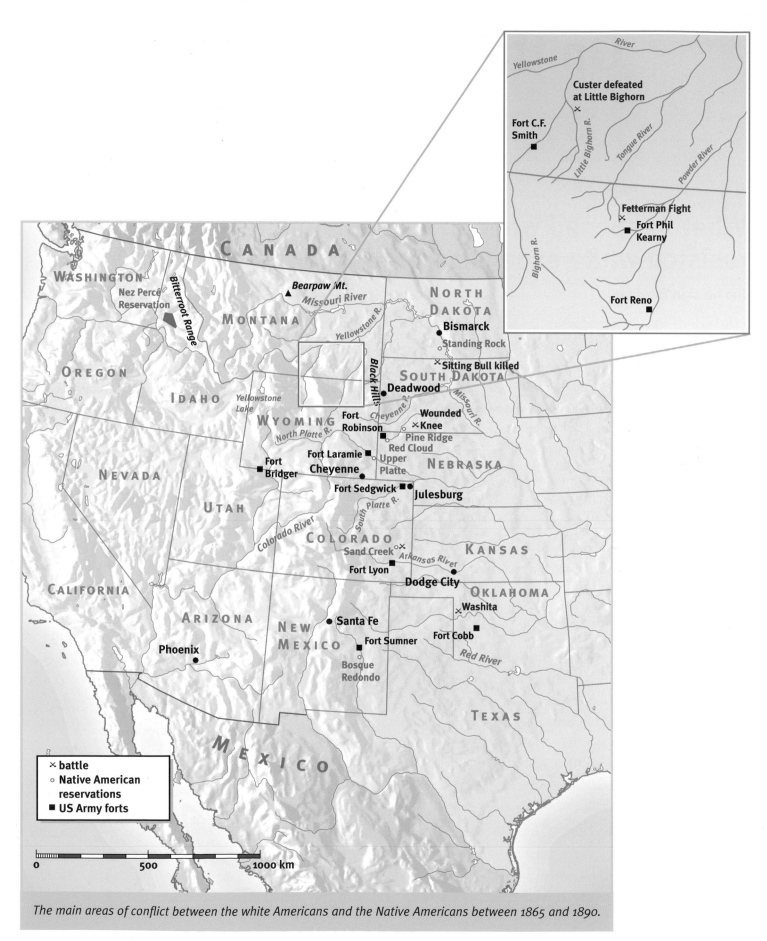

The main areas of conflict between the white Americans and the Native Americans between 1865 and 1890.

SOURCE A

Cheyenne and Arapaho chiefs in September 1864. Black Kettle sits in the middle of the front row. Silas Soule, who refused to take part in the Sand Creek massacre, is kneeling to the right.

The Navaho

In 1864, 6000 Navaho were escorted to the Bosque Redondo reservation near Fort Sumner in New Mexico. Conditions on the reservation were dreadful. The Navaho had a tradition of farming, but they could do nothing with that land. Many starved. Even General Sherman, who had little time for Native Americans, was appalled when he saw their situation. The way the Navaho were treated was a foretaste of things to come for the Plains Indians.

The Sand Creek massacre

During the 1860s, there were a series of conflicts between the US army and the Cheyenne and Arapaho on the central Plains. Further south, the Comanche and Kiowa fought to protect their lands. The immediate cause of tension was the discovery of gold at Pike's Peak near Denver, Colorado. The tide of white people moving into Colorado led the US government to think again about the terms of the 1851 Fort Laramie Treaty.

In February 1861, Cheyenne and Arapaho chiefs were persuaded to give up the lands granted to them at Fort Laramie. Under the terms of the Treaty of Fort Lyon (sometimes known as Fort Wise), they were given a smaller reservation at Sand Creek, near the River Arkansas in Colorado. Many Cheyenne people could not accept this. Between 1861 and 1864, they attacked mining camps, mail coaches, settlers and travellers.

John Evans, the governor of Colorado, decided that this meant that a state of war existed between the Native Americans and the whites. He recruited a militia under the command of Colonel John M. Chivington, a former Methodist preacher. The militia were a bunch of tough characters from the mines and saloon bars around Denver.

The leader of the Cheyenne was Black Kettle. He was a peaceful man who believed in compromise. Black Kettle realised that a state of continual war was not likely to benefit his people, and he wanted to negotiate a peace. On 28 September 1864, he met with Evans and Chivington. Believing that peace had been secured, he led his tribe back to Sand Creek.

SOURCE B

ATTENTION! INDIAN FIGHTERS

Having been authorized by the Governor to raise a Company of 100 day

U. S. VOL CAVALRY!

For immediate service against hostile Indians. I call upon all who wish to engage in such service to call at my office and enroll their names immediately.

Pay and Rations the same as other U. S. Volunteer Cavalry.

Parties furnishing their own horses will receive 40c per day, and rations for the same, while in the service.

The Company will also be entitled to all horses and other plunder taken from the Indians.

Office first door East of Recorder's Office.

HAL SAYR.

Central City, Aug. 13, '64.

Posters like this one from 1864 asked for volunteers for Chivington's militia.

Chivington had other ideas. He decided to attack Black Kettle's village. When one officer protested, Chivington replied: 'Damn any man who sympathises with Indians! I have come to kill Indians, and believe it is right and honourable to use any means under God's heaven to kill Indians.' Early on the morning of 29 November, Chivington and his men surrounded the settlement at Sand Creek. Most of the Native Americans were still asleep. Black Kettle was puzzled, but did not think there could be any danger — the two sides were supposed to have made peace. The chief did what he had always been advised to do in such a situation: he raised the US flag and a white flag over his tepee to indicate that the Native Americans had no wish to fight.

The raising of the US flag made no difference. The army charged into the camp. Men, women and children were slaughtered. It was a dreadful, unprovoked attack — one of the worst in the history of the West. Estimates of the number of people killed vary, but it is generally thought to have been around 450. Two-thirds of these were women and children.

SOURCE C

George Bent was the son of a white trader and a Cheyenne woman. He was at the Sand Creek massacre, and described the scene:

When I looked towards the chief's lodge, I saw that Black Kettle had a large US flag up on a long lodgepole as a signal to the troop that the camp was friendly. Part of the warriors were running out towards the pony herds and the rest of the people were rushing around the camp in great fear. All the time Black Kettle kept calling out not to be frightened: that the camp was under protection and there was no danger.

D. Brown, *Bury My Heart at Wounded Knee*, 1970

SOURCE D

The trader John Smith also witnessed the massacre:

They were scalped, their brains knocked out; the men used their knives, ripped open women, clubbed little children, knocked them in the head with their guns, beat their brains out, mutilated their bodies in every sense of the word.

R. A. Billington and M. Ridge, *Westward Expansion*, 1949

SOURCE E

Colonel John M. Chivington. It is said he talked of 'collecting scalps' and 'wading in gore'.

SOURCE F

The Sand Creek Massacre, *painted by Robert Lindneux in 1936. The raised US flag is clearly shown.*

Black Kettle escaped after the massacre and eventually headed south. Even the US government condemned what had happened at Sand Creek. Chivington, though, was never charged with any crime. A soldier called Silas Soule who had refused to participate in the massacre was mysteriously murdered after testifying against Chivington.

News of the massacre at Sand Creek inevitably provoked the Cheyenne and their allies into retaliation. The 'dog soldiers', the most important Cheyenne warriors, took matters into their own hands. They attacked settlements and supply wagons and tore down telegraph wires. At one stage, Denver was completely cut off.

Two Civil War heroes of the Union, General William T. Sherman and General Philip H. Sheridan, were brought west to subdue the Cheyenne. Both generals were violently prejudiced against the Native Americans, and they were to play a prominent part in subsequent Indian campaigns. War spread across the Great Plains, to the north and south. Sand Creek had brought the Plains Indian tribes closer together. To the north, the Cheyenne teamed up with the Sioux. To the south, the Comanche and Kiowa joined the battle.

The Medicine Lodge Creek Treaty 1867

Eventually, an attempt was made to end the war on the central and southern Plains. US government officials met with the representatives of 5000 Plains Indians (Cheyenne, Arapaho, Comanche, Kiowa and Kiowa–Apache) who had gathered at Medicine Lodge Creek in Kansas. They agreed a treaty that established two reservations in the Indian Territory, one for the Cheyenne and Arapaho, and another for the Comanche, Kiowa and Kiowa–Apache. The Native Americans were to be given schooling, instruction in farming, and gifts of regular clothing and food. In short, they agreed to give up their traditional hunting way of life.

This seemed like total defeat for the Native Americans. The chiefs accepted the terms because men such as Black Kettle were beginning to realise that the Native Americans could not continue their way of life as before. The white soldiers had better weapons, and the buffalo stocks were rapidly diminishing.

The Medicine Lodge Creek Treaty did not bring peace to the southern Plains. Many warriors, especially the younger ones, simply could not accept the terms of the treaty. By August 1868, several Great Plains tribes were on the warpath again. Sherman and Sheridan were ordered to tackle the problem. Sheridan thought that the solution was a winter campaign, because the Plains Indians rarely fought in winter.

The Battle of Washita

In November 1868, the US army reached the Washita Valley in the Indian Territory, where some of the warring Cheyenne and Arapaho were camped. The main US force was the Seventh Cavalry, led by General George Custer. On 27 November, Custer rushed upon the sleeping Indian camp as the army band played his favourite tune, *Garry Owen*. Over 100 Cheyenne and Arapaho were killed, including Black Kettle.

Two months later, the remaining Cheyenne and Arapaho chiefs signed a new agreement at Fort Cobb. They agreed to stay on a reservation on the upper Washita River. The Kiowa and the Comanche were sent to the lands allotted to them by the Medicine Lodge Creek Treaty.

The Red River War

The last major outbreak of resistance on the southern Plains took place in 1874/75. Kiowa and Comanche warriors clashed with the US army in what became known as the Red River War. The Kiowa chief Satanta was arrested. Satanta was tried, found guilty and sentenced to be hanged. Satanta's case, though, became famous across the whole country, and public pressure caused the governor of Texas to pardon him.

Satanta's release did not end the conflict. A further 3000 US troops were sent in, and by 1875 the resistance was over. The surviving Native Americans returned wearily to their reservations.

Red Cloud's war

In the early 1860s, gold was discovered in Montana. Any miner wanting to travel to that remote part of the West faced a big problem: there was no direct road to the gold fields. The US government was keen to open up Montana to economic development. In 1866, a decision was taken to build a new road, the Bozeman Trail, through the Powder River country.

The route cut through the heart of Sioux hunting grounds. The land was, in theory at least, protected under the terms of the 1851 Fort Laramie Treaty. The Sioux chief Red Cloud was strongly opposed to the new road. His opposition grew fiercer still when the US army, commanded by Colonel Carrington, began the construction of three forts along the route: Fort Reno, Fort Phil Kearny and Fort C. F. Smith.

SOURCE G

Red Cloud responded angrily to the encroachment on the Sioux hunting grounds:

The white men have crowded the Indians back year by year until we are forced to live in a small country north of the Platte, and now our last hunting ground, the home of the People, is to be taken from us. Our women and children will starve, but for my part I prefer to die fighting than by starvation.

D. Brown, *Bury My Heart at Wounded Knee*, 1970

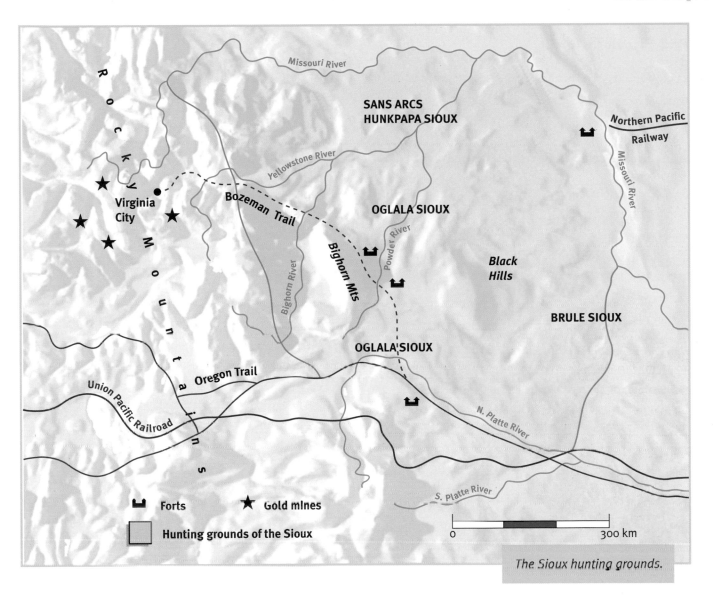

The Sioux hunting grounds.

The decision of the Sioux to fight hard for their hunting grounds was also influenced by the execution of the Santee in Minnesota and the Sand Creek massacre.

As the new forts were being built on Sioux territory, the US troops came under continual attack. Carrington's policy was to defend himself against the raids and complete the work as quickly as possible. Others, such as Captain William J. Fetterman, favoured a more aggressive line. On 21 December 1866, the Native Americans attacked a train carrying timber. Fetterman headed an 80-strong group of reinforcements. Defying Carrington's orders, he rode straight into an ambush. The men were surrounded by nearly 2000 Sioux warriors. All of them lost their lives. The incident become known as the Fetterman Fight, or Fetterman massacre.

Before the end of 1868, Red Cloud's war was over. A second Fort Laramie Treaty was agreed and, for once, the Native American side won some significant concessions from the US government. In return for an end to the fighting, the whole of South Dakota west of the Missouri was set aside as the Great Sioux Reservation. The area included the sacred Black Hills. The three forts were abandoned, and work on the road was stopped.

THREE SIOUX CHIEFS

Red Cloud

Red Cloud came from the Oglala branch of the Teton Sioux. His main strengths were in planning and organising, rather than in being a great warrior.

Red Cloud photographed in 1880.

After his victories over the US army seemed to have secured the Sioux homelands, he returned to Powder River country to live with his people. When it became obvious that the terms of the 1868 Fort Laramie Treaty were not being kept by the whites, the Sioux turned to younger men such as Crazy Horse and Sitting Bull. In later years, Red Cloud reluctantly accepted reservation life. He died in 1909 at the age of 87.

Crazy Horse

Like Red Cloud, Crazy Horse was an Oglala Sioux. Unlike Red Cloud, Crazy Horse liked to be at the forefront of a battle. It was Crazy Horse who lured Fetterman to his death in 1866.

Throughout his life, Crazy Horse fought hard for his people's right to stay in their homelands. He played a great part in defeating Custer at Little Bighorn in 1876. A year later, he surrendered and went to live on a reservation. It was rumoured that he planned to escape, and he was arrested and taken to Fort Robinson. When he saw that he was to be locked in a cell, he resisted. During the struggle, he was stabbed to death with a bayonet. Crazy Horse remains a mysterious figure. There is no known photograph of him, and his place of burial is a secret.

Sitting Bull

Sitting Bull was a chief of the Hunkpapa Sioux. He was also a greatly respected religious man. After he became the leader of the whole of the Teton Sioux, he urged that the white man must be resisted at all costs. Sitting Bull's authority was such that large numbers of Cheyenne and Arapaho as well as Sioux gathered together at the Little Bighorn to fight Custer. Before the battle, he had a vision which showed Custer's defeat. During the battle, he remained in his camp praying.

Sitting Bull (1831–90).

After the Battle of Little Bighorn, Sitting Bull fled to Canada. He later returned and surrendered in 1881, and went to live on a reservation. For a time, he joined *Buffalo Bill's Wild West*, a kind of circus which attempted to portray aspects of Western life. This must have been a humiliating experience for such a proud man. In 1890, he was arrested by US forces concerned about Sioux unrest, and was shot dead by police when an attempt was made to rescue him.

>> Activities

1 Construct a detailed timeline showing what happened in the conflicts between Native Americans and white Americans between 1860 and 1875. Indicate whether you think that each event on the timeline was a Native American victory or a white American victory.

2 What does the Sand Creek massacre tell us about how US army officers viewed the Native Americans?

The Battle of Little Bighorn and its aftermath

The conflicts with the Native Americans did not die down after the battles and treaties of the 1860s. The whites still took Indian land whenever they wanted it. Many Native Americans could not resign themselves to life on the reservations, where the conditions were appalling.

What brought an end to Native American resistance in the West?

Gold in the Black Hills

For several years in the middle of the nineteenth century, rumours circulated that there was gold in the Black Hills of Dakota. In 1874, the US government asked General Custer to organise a survey of the area to see if this was true. This was bound to provoke the Sioux and their allies, because the Black Hills were on Sioux land. Custer was loathed by the Plains Indians, and now he was intruding on sacred land.

The existence of gold was confirmed, and thousands of miners poured into the Black Hills. All over the country, newspapers urged their readers to head for South Dakota. The rights of the Sioux, and the terms of the 1868 Fort Laramie Treaty, were conveniently forgotten. The government tried to buy the land from the Sioux, but the offer was rejected. It made little difference. The settlers started mining and building towns as though the land belonged to them anyway.

In the meantime, large numbers of Sioux led by Sitting Bull and Crazy Horse were still living in the Powder River country. They had never accepted the terms of the 1868 Fort Laramie Treaty. The US government ordered them to return to the Black Hills reservation. They refused, and the US army was sent in to make them comply with the order.

SOURCE A

An impression of the Battle of Little Bighorn by the Lakota artist Kicking Bear who was a warrior in the battle. Where is Custer here?

The Battle of Little Bighorn

In the early summer of 1876, some 7000 followers of Sitting Bull and Crazy Horse were camped in the valley of a river called the Little Bighorn in present-day Montana. It was here that General Sheridan decided to strike. His plan was for the US troops to move towards the Little Bighorn river from three different directions. General Crook marched north from Fort Fetterman with 1000 men. General Gibbon came in from Fort Ellis to the west. The third column was commanded by General Terry, and it came from Fort Abraham Lincoln near Bismarck in North Dakota. Terry's forces included the Seventh Cavalry under the leadership of General Custer.

On 17 June, Crook ran into a large party of Sioux and Cheyenne warriors at Rosebud Creek. After six hours of heavy fighting, he was forced to retreat. The three-pronged attack was starting to fail. Four days later, Terry and Gibbon met up. They did not know that Crook had been forced to turn back. However, they did know that the Sioux were camped in the Little Bighorn valley. A plan was devised in which Custer would head south down Rosebud Creek. He would then cross to the valley of the Little Bighorn and turn north. Meanwhile, Terry and Gibbon would position themselves at the north end of the Little Bighorn valley. The Sioux would then be trapped between the two sets of troops.

The plan might have succeeded had it not been for Custer. He was a vain man, who had once boasted that he could defeat the entire Sioux nation with one regiment. He was eager for glory, and wanted to repeat his 'triumph' at the massacre at Washita. Although his orders were to detain the Native Americans until Terry arrived, he decided to go on the attack.

Custer had around 600 men, divided into three groups. One group of 125 men under the command of Captain Fred Benteen entered the Little Bighorn valley from the south. The second division, under Major Reno, advanced towards the Indian camp from a position west of Benteen's. Reno's forces were badly defeated, but were saved from complete destruction by the arrival of Benteen. Meanwhile, Custer was determined to rout the Sioux with his own band of 265 men. His scouts had warned him that the Indian camp was huge, but Custer took no notice of their advice. In fact, 2500 warriors lay in wait for him. Custer was spotted on the hills high above the valley. He was soon surrounded by Sioux and Cheyenne warriors. Chief Gall of the Sioux, who had defeated Reno, attacked from the south. Crazy Horse and his warriors looped round from the north.

SOURCE B

Custer's Last Fight, *depicted by Otto Becker in 1896. What kind of impression does this give of Custer? How does Becker's view of the battle differ from that of Kicking Bear in Source A?*

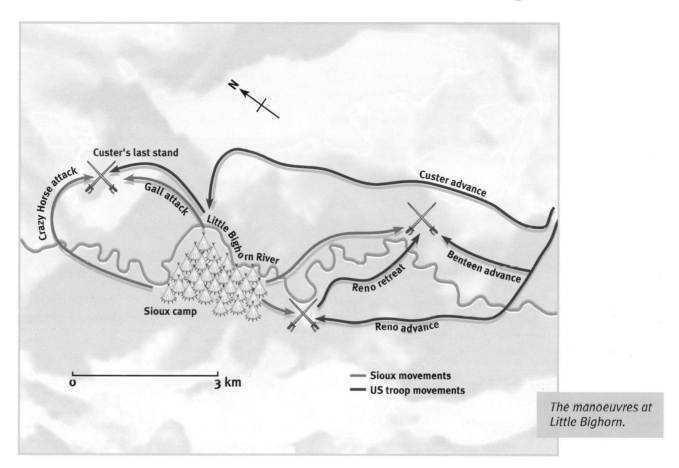

Sioux movements
US troop movements

The manoeuvres at Little Bighorn.

The result was the biggest single defeat of the US army in the history of the West. Not one of Custer's soldiers survived. They were defeated by superior numbers of warriors who were better armed with the latest repeating rifles, and the foolishness of Custer's tactics. No-one knows for certain exactly how Custer himself died. One theory is that he killed himself before the Native Americans could reach him. His body had not been touched, and the Sioux did not mutilate those who had committed suicide.

GEORGE ARMSTRONG CUSTER

Custer was one of the most controversial figures in the history of the West. He was born in Ohio in 1839. From an early age, he wanted to follow a military career. He gained a place at the United States Military Academy at West Point. He was known for his undisciplined behaviour even then, and he came bottom of his class.

Custer distinguished himself on the side of the Union in the Civil War. After the war, he joined the Seventh Cavalry, and led a series of campaigns against the Plains Indians. He was not popular with his troops. In 1867, he was court-martialled and suspended from duty because of his harsh treatment of them.

Custer was an immature and arrogant man who liked to pose for photographs. He generally wore buckskin trousers, which became his trademark, and he wore his hair long. His attitude towards the Plains Indians was contradictory. He admired their freedom of spirit, but at the same time described them as 'treacherous' and 'bloodthirsty'. He believed that no mercy could be shown towards them, and he thought that those who supported them were 'sentimental'.

Shortly before the Battle of Little Bighorn, Custer was rebuked by the US President, Ulysses S. Grant, for testifying against Grant's brother in a court case. Custer was keen to restore his good name, and this may have been one of the reasons for his reckless behaviour in the battle.

After the Battle of Little Bighorn

In 1876, the American nation was busy celebrating its centenary: it was exactly 100 years since the American Declaration of Independence. A world's fair was in full swing in Philadelphia. When the news of Custer's Last Stand reached the East, a confident nation was stunned. Newspapers told of a massacre and demanded revenge.

SOURCE C

In July 1876, Congressman Maginnis summed up the feelings of many:

The blood of our soldiers demands that these Indians shall be pursued. They must submit themselves to the authority of the nation.

C. F. Taylor and W. C. Sturtevant, *The Native Americans*, 1996

The reaction of the Plains Indians was very different. They rejoiced in their glorious victory. Sitting Bull's great vision had come true. In reality, though, the Battle of Little Bighorn was the beginning of the end for the Plains Indians and their way of life.

>> Activity

1 Was Custer's character

   a the only reason

   b the main reason

   c one of several reasons for his defeat at the Battle of Little Bighorn? Explain your choice.

The collapse of the Native American forces

The victory at the Little Bighorn was not repeated. By the end of October 1876, the Sioux war army had been forced to disband. The majority surrendered and went back to the reservation in South Dakota.

The northern Cheyenne who had fought at Little Bighorn were sent to a reservation in the Indian Territory. In 1878, led by Dull Knife, they tried to return to their hunting grounds. Many died on the march north. Cold and hunger forced them to surrender, but they were eventually allowed to settle on reservations in Montana.

Reservation life

After 1876, there was no prospect of a Native American military victory against the whites. The only option for the Plains Indians was life on a reservation, but many found this hard to accept. They were hunters, not farmers. Their plight was made worse by the fact that the reservations were so badly run. Most of the government agents were unsympathetic to the Native Americans. They had a great deal of power, and little respect for traditional Native American customs and practices. Food rations were often inadequate, as were medical supplies.

The Plains Indians were not given the resources they needed to succeed as farmers. They were given less than 1 acre of land each to farm. This was completely inadequate. Like the white settlers, they also had to contend with drought, plagues of grasshoppers, and other hardships. Efforts were made to destroy Native American culture by educating Native American children in European-style schools and attempting to convert them to Christianity.

The 1887 Dawes Act

Most whites argued that the only solution to the Native American problem was for the Native Americans to adopt the white American way of life.

SOURCE D

Thomas Jefferson Morgan, Commissioner of Indian Affairs, summed up the view of the US government:

The Indians must conform to the 'white man's ways', peaceably if they will, forcibly if they must. They must adjust themselves to their environment, and conform their mode of living substantially to our civilization.

A. M. Josephy, *500 Nations*, 1995

The US government decided to break up much of the reservation land in order to create bigger private farms for Native American families. The Dawes Act of 1887 gave 160 acres to the head of any Native American family who wanted to farm. Those taking up the offer would become citizens of the USA.

These plots of land did not go directly to the Native Americans. They were held in trust by the government for 25 years. The idea was to prevent the new owners from selling their land to white settlers. It failed to prevent widespread fraud. Corrupt agents even went so far as to register horses and dogs as landowners before selling the land to whites.

The Oklahoma Land Rush

By the 1880s, white settlers were looking jealously at the large reservation on the southern Plains known as the Indian Territory. Some took the law into their own hands and seized land for themselves. They were known as 'Boomers'. In 1889, the US government decided to give in to the pressure. The US President, Benjamin Harrison, announced that the Oklahoma District would be opened up to white settlers at noon on 22 April.

As the hour approached, excitement reached fever pitch. 100,000 people lined up around the borders of the territory. At 12.00, shots were fired in the air, and the race was on. Wagons and horses charged forward and men leapt from trains. All were desperate to stake out a claim on vacant land. After just a few hours, the Oklahoma District was settled. The boundaries of Oklahoma City were established by the end of the day.

The last flickerings of resistance

The Nez Percé tribe lived in Oregon. In 1877, their leader, Chief Joseph, led a last heroic campaign against the US army. The Native Americans finally surrendered near the Canadian border after marching 1000 miles and fighting a rearguard action. In the 1880s, the Apaches in Arizona and New Mexico, led by Geronimo, resisted the army. Geronimo finally surrendered in 1886.

The Ghost Dance

In 1890, the situation of the Sioux on the South Dakota reservations seemed worse than ever. Their rations, already low, were cut. Disease was rife. At the Pine Ridge reservation, people were dying at a rate of about 35 a month. Many of these were small children. To make matters worse, the harvest failed.

SOURCE E

The Sioux Reservation at Pine Ridge, South Dakota, in about 1890. The tents and utensils were supplied by the government.

SOURCE F

Arapaho women performing a ghost dance.

A rumour began to spread among the Sioux of a messiah, someone with magical powers who would end their troubles and restore their power. A Native American called Wovoka who lived far away in Nevada was seen as this messiah. He said that if the Plains Indians adopted a new dance then all the whites would disappear, the buffalo would return, and everyone could resume their old way of life. The dance was called the Ghost Dance.

Some Native American leaders, such as Sitting Bull, were dubious about Wovoka and the Ghost Dance. The Ghost Dance was not a traditional ceremony like the Sun Dance. Wovoka was a shaman (a holy man), but he had lived with a white family for some time, and had even been given an English name: Jack Wilson.

However, these were desperate times for the Sioux. Many took up the new belief with great enthusiasm. They danced on and on, in some cases until they were unconscious. They claimed to have actually visited the spirit world and seen their dead friends and relatives. The authorities became alarmed. To them, this was not a religious revival, but a dangerous outbreak of mad defiance.

SOURCE G

One Sioux woman called Ella Deloria later wrote about the Ghost Dance:

The people went on and on and could not stop day or night, hoping to get a vision of their own dead. And so I suppose the authorities did think they were crazy – but they weren't. They were only terribly unhappy.

E. Deloria, *Speaking of Indians*, 1944

SOURCE H

The Wounded Knee Massacre: the frozen body of Chief Big Foot lies in the snow.

The massacre at Wounded Knee

By November 1890, the Ghost Dance was sweeping across the reservations at Pine Ridge and Rosebud in South Dakota. Some of the dancers wore 'ghost shirts', which they thought would protect them against the bullets of the white man.

The government agent at the Pine Ridge reservation was a weak man called Daniel Royer. He called in the US army. This heightened the tension. Sitting Bull was killed by a member of the Indian Police in December, and feelings then ran even higher. On 29 December 1890, a band of Minneconjou Sioux led by Big Foot were surrounded by the Seventh Cavalry at Wounded Knee Creek. The Sioux were asked to disarm and agreed to do so. The troops, though, were nervous, unsettled by the atmosphere created by the Ghost Dance. A rifle went off and fighting broke out. In the confusion, the troops opened fire with four cannons. 146 Sioux were killed, including over 60 women and children.

The massacre of Wounded Knee has come to be seen as the last great act of violence against the Plains Indians. Some say the army did not mean to open fire. Others say they went there intending to kill. All agree that it was a terrible end to a bitter series of conflicts.

>> Activities

1 How successful was the 1887 Dawes Act in helping Native Americans?

2 Why did so many Native Americans stop fighting the white Americans and join the Ghost Dancers?

3 Was the fighting at Wounded Knee Creek in 1890 a battle or a massacre? Explain your answer.

The war for the Great Plains

THE OUTBREAK OF FIGHTING

> On the Great Plains, both the Native Americans and the whites claimed ownership of the land. The Native Americans had lived in the West for hundreds of years. The US government wanted there to be one American nation stretching from the Atlantic to the Pacific.

> The advance of the homesteaders, mining developments, the railroad and the destruction of the buffalo herds all caused friction and heightened tension on the Great Plains.

> After some fighting, the 1851 Fort Laramie Treaty gave the main Plains Indian tribes the right to live on their own reservations without interference. Settlers were not to be allowed on those lands.

> The US army continued to be extremely hostile towards the Native Americans. The US government made repeated attempts to force the Native Americans onto reservations.

THE BEGINNING OF THE INDIAN WARS

> The tensions exploded into a series of battles and killings across the Great Plains in the 1860s. In 1862, 38 Santee Sioux were executed in Minnesota. There was a terrible massacre of Native Americans at Sand Creek, Colorado, in 1864.

> The 1867 Medicine Lodge Creek Treaty established new Indian reservations on the southern Plains, but this did not bring peace. The 1874 Red River War was the last outbreak of resistance in the south.

> In the north west, after conflict over the building of a new road, the Bozeman Trail, through Sioux territory in Montana, the 1868 Fort Laramie Treaty established a huge new Sioux reservation in South Dakota.

THE BATTLE OF LITTLE BIGHORN AND THE END OF NATIVE AMERICAN RESISTANCE

> In the early 1870s, there was Sioux unrest because of the discovery of gold in the sacred Black Hills of South Dakota and a flood of miners into the area. In 1876, the US army was sent to force Sioux living in Montana to move to the South Dakota reservation.

> The Sioux were camped in the Little Bighorn river valley. US army forces advanced on them from several directions. General Custer and his troop of 265 men were cut off and surrounded by Sioux warriors. All the soldiers were killed.

> The Native Americans were ecstatic about their great victory, but the American nation was outraged, and demanded vengeance. The battle marked the beginning of the end for the way of life of the Plains Indians. By the end of the year, the Sioux army had been forced to disband.

> Further Native American resistance was crushed, and the Native Americans were forced into unsuitable reservations with inadequate resources. Efforts were made to destroy their culture. The whites took over more Indian land in Oklahoma in 1889.

> In 1890, the Sioux in South Dakota began to dance the Ghost Dance in a desperate attempt to re-create their past. The craze swept across the Great Plains and greatly alarmed the authorities. Tension increased.

> Frightened by the unrest, the government agent at the Sioux Pine Ridge reservation called in the US army. The Seventh Cavalry surrounded and disarmed a band of Minneconjou Sioux at Wounded Knee Creek. Fighting broke out, and 146 Sioux men, women and children were massacred. This was the last great act of violence against the Plains Indians. The spirit of the Native Americans had finally been broken.

>> Review question

The wars on the Great Plains have been described by some white historians as the 'Indian Problem'. Do you agree or disagree with this interpretation?

Law and order

Western films suggest that the West was a particularly violent and criminal place in the nineteenth century. Historians believe that this view is exaggerated. Nevertheless, there was a law and order problem.

Why was crime and disorder so common in the West?

To most people today, the American West means the Wild West. Wyatt Earp, Butch Cassidy, Wild Bill Hickok, Calamity Jane and Billy the Kid are familiar names. They were first made famous by the 'dime novels': cheap popular stories in which the West was depicted as exciting and violent.

Hollywood films started presenting this image of the West in the early twentieth century, and the tradition has continued more or less up to the present day. Even now, films portray the West as a lawless place where sheriffs, marshals and outlaws frequently come into conflict.

The wildness of the West has probably been exaggerated. The total number of violent deaths in the West, apart from those in the Indian conflicts and massacres, was small. As the nineteenth century progressed, schools, churches and banks were as much a feature of the new towns as saloons or bars. Nevertheless, guns and rifles were part of everyday life. For a few years, mining towns such as Tombstone and Deadwood were violent places. Dodge City had a bad reputation in its early years.

The West developed very quickly. The speed of settlement made it difficult to govern. Mining towns and cattle towns sprang up almost overnight without officials to govern them.

SOURCE A

Dime novels introduced a wide reading public to the West. The cover of this one shows Billy the Kid. Some thought him a hero, but others saw him as a worthless outlaw.

HOW THE WEST WAS GOVERNED

In the nineteenth century, the USA had two systems of government: federal government and state government. The federal government was based in Washington DC. It was headed by the US president, who was elected every four years. The people of the USA also elected members of Congress, which consisted of two chambers: the Senate and the House of Representatives.

The federal government took decisions on matters that affected the whole nation, such as defence and overseas trade. The individual states of the USA also had considerable power to make their own laws. They were responsible for such matters as law and order and education. Each state had its own capital and governor.

When new land was absorbed into the USA, it became a US 'territory'. It was often many years before territories became states. A territory had to have at least 60,000 inhabitants before it could apply to become a state. Until that time, the governor and top officials were appointed by the federal government. Territories and states were further subdivided into counties and towns for the purposes of local government.

Some territories, such as Oklahoma, New Mexico and Arizona, did not become states until the twentieth century. They therefore had to rely on the federal government to run most of their affairs. This often meant that decisions were delayed. In the early years, transport in the West was slow, and this limited the ability of the federal government to control what went on far from Washington DC. The sheer size of the West also made it hard for the federal government to act quickly and effectively.

The West was a place where individuals went to make a name for themselves. Some of these people were ruthless, and nothing was going to stand in their way. Owners of large corporations were ready to use violence and hire gunmen to protect their interests. This was especially true of some of the large cattle barons. This led to several 'range wars' in which gunmen paid by the cattle barons fought with homesteaders and smaller ranchers.

Law enforcement officers were not easy to find. They also varied greatly in quality. Sheriffs and marshals were often former criminals. Some carried on their illegal activities after they became lawmen.

Henry Plummer was the sheriff of Bannack in the Montana gold fields. He headed a gang called the Innocents, and embarked on a spree of robberies and murders. In the absence of effective law and order, some people, known as 'vigilantes', took the law into their own hands. A vigilante group caught and hanged 20 of Henry Plummer's gang, including the sheriff himself.

While vigilantes often dealt with genuine criminals, they also attacked innocent people and were used to settle arguments and grievances.

SOURCE B

A victim of vigilante justice.

LAW ENFORCEMENT OFFICERS

US marshals

US marshals were federal law officers who were appointed by the authority of the US president. Marshals had authority over territories or states. They were responsible for bringing to court people suspected of serious federal crimes such as robbing mail trains. They also dealt with crimes committed on Indian reservations and US army deserters. Marshals appointed deputy marshals to assist them. These officers were responsible for a smaller area such as a county or town.

Sheriffs and town marshals

There were also local law enforcement officers. A sheriff was like a local policeman, and he was appointed by the county. Some places also had town marshals. Sheriffs and town marshals dealt with minor law and order issues such as fights and brawls. Both sheriffs and town marshals could also act as deputy marshals.

Texas Rangers

In Texas, there was an additional group of law enforcement officers known as the Texas Rangers. This force was first formed when Texas was part of Mexico, but they later fought in the war of independence against the Mexicans. Their main role was to protect white people against Native Americans, particularly the Comanche. The Texas Rangers also acted as a police force against outlaws. They were quite independent of the authorities; they wore no uniform, and they even provided their own firearms and horses.

Private detectives

Private detective agencies flourished in this period. The most famous of these was the Pinkerton Detective Agency. This was founded by Allan Pinkerton, a Scotsman. The agency played an important role in fighting crime all over the West. However, the Pinkerton Detective Agency was not popular. It gained a reputation for breaking mining and railroad strikes.

Deadwood: law and order in a mining town

Deadwood was the best known of the South Dakota mining towns. In 1876, 7000 miners rushed there after gold had been found in the Black Hills. For a brief period, Deadwood was notorious.

Jack McCall was a drifter. On 2 August 1876, he wandered into Nuttall and Mann's saloon in the town of Deadwood. There he saw Wild Bill Hickok playing poker with his back to the door. McCall calmly shot Hickok in the back of the head. In his defence, he claimed that Wild Bill had killed his brother. This was Deadwood's most infamous murder.

Opinions vary as to how lawless Deadwood really was.

SOURCE C

Nathan Butler, a citizen of Deadwood, described the town in 1877:

Full of crooks of all kinds – gamblers, confidence men, pickpockets, thieves, highwaymen, and murderers.

Just six years later, the Deadwood Times *saw Deadwood differently:*

Deadwood is one of the most moral and best behaved mining towns in the west.

W. Parker, *Deadwood – The Golden Years,* 1981

SOURCE D

Downtown Deadwood at the height of its fame.

Statistics provide contradictory information about Deadwood. The coroner of Lawrence County (of which Deadwood was a part) recorded only three murders between 1877 and 1898. Other evidence suggests that there were 16 murders in Lawrence County during 1878 alone. There are two possible reasons for the inconsistencies:

> For a few years after the big mining boom in 1876, crime in Deadwood was at its height. As the town settled down, the crime rate dropped.

> Most of the violent crimes were committed by criminals against criminals, and this meant that they were often not recorded. Much of it also took place outside the boundaries of the town.

Everyone agrees that Deadwood was a rough and lively place. In 1877, a person could choose to visit any of 75 saloons, wandering from the Little Bonanza to the Red Bird to the Old Crow. On one day, the *Deadwood Times* noted 14 drunks on the street. Gambling was another cause of quarrels which often erupted in violence.

Stagecoach robberies were common. The Northwestern Stage Transportation Company made its passengers exchange their money for bank drafts before the start of a journey.

SOURCE E

Charles M. Russell's In Without Knocking *(1909) is based on a real incident in Stanford, Montana. The five cowboys did not bother to dismount at the end of their trail drive.*

Dodge City: law and order in a cattle town

There is a story that a young cowboy was heading west on a Kansas Pacific train in 1874. When the conductor asked him where he was going, the cowboy replied that he was going to hell. The conductor smiled, and gave him a ticket for Dodge City. The tale may or may not be true, but it shows what a reputation Dodge City had for violence in the early 1870s.

During this time, Dodge City was dominated by buffalo hunters, and the town became disreputable. When it became a cattle town, the local businessmen wanted the law to be more strictly enforced. In 1881, an attempt was made to ban alcohol in the town, and an anti-alcohol campaigner called Alonzo B. Webster was elected mayor.

Even in its most lively period, Dodge City had only eight taverns and two dance halls, as compared with Deadwood's 75 saloons.

Like the other Kansas cattle towns, Dodge City was a place where cowboys came to have a good time after their hard work on the trails or roundups. Sometimes the result was fighting and disorder, but the town was no more violent than many other places. Vigilante justice was rare in Dodge City; it was only recorded once, in 1881. Between 1870 and 1885, only 45 men were killed in all of the Kansas cattle towns, and 16 of these were killed by law officers. This is a far cry from the shoot-outs so often seen in Western films.

WYATT EARP

Wyatt Earp was born in Illinois in 1848. After working as a freight hauler and a buffalo hunter, he became a deputy marshal in Wichita, Kansas, in 1875. He moved to Dodge City in 1876, and was made assistant marshal there in 1878.

Wyatt Earp's main claim to fame rests on the time he spent in Tombstone, Arizona, where his brother Virgil was a deputy marshal. Wyatt became deputy sheriff of the county. Tombstone was best known for its silver mines, but it was also a centre for ranching, and this attracted many cattle rustlers. Earp identified himself closely with the local business community. They were keen to establish Tombstone as a respectable town and put an end to the rustling and violence. Two families, the Clantons and the McLaurys, were thought to be the cause of most of the trouble.

The showdown came on 26 October 1881. This was the famous gunfight at the OK Corral. The shooting actually lasted less than 1 minute, but two of the McLaury brothers and Billy Clanton were killed. Some said the Earps had killed them in cold blood. The fight did not stop the violence. Morgan Earp, another of Wyatt's brothers, was shot dead the following year. Wyatt Earp sought to avenge his murder, and eventually shot the two men suspected of the crime.

Wyatt Earp had a long and eventful life, and died in 1929 aged 80. In his last years, he helped to turn himself into a legend by telling his life story to writers and Hollywood film makers.

Wyatt Earp. He took part in the gunfight at the OK Corral.

BAT MASTERSON

Bat Masterson, another lawman and a friend of Wyatt Earp.

Like many lawmen, Bat Masterson had a colourful career. At various times he was a buffalo hunter, a gambler and a sports journalist. Masterson moved to Dodge City in 1876, and became county sheriff. His brother Ed, a town marshal, was killed by a drunken cowhand in Dodge City two years later. He became closely associated with Wyatt Earp and even moved to Tombstone for a while. He was later appointed as a New York State deputy marshal by President Theodore Roosevelt.

WILD BILL HICKOK

Wild Bill Hickok's real name was James Butler Hickok. He earned his nickname in the Civil War, and he continued to serve in the US army for a few years after the war as a scout. He was one gunfighter and lawman who fully deserved his fearsome reputation. By the time he was appointed town marshal of Hays, Kansas, in 1869, he had already killed a number of men. After his time in Hays, he became a marshal in Abilene.

Hickok arrived in Deadwood in 1876. Many hoped that he would bring law and order to the town, but he decided to bide his time. He gambled in the saloons, got married, and thought about gold mining until he was eventually shot while playing poker.

JESSE JAMES

Jesse James was born in Missouri in 1847, the son of a Baptist minister. Together with his brother Frank he formed the James gang, which often teamed up with the four Younger brothers. Between 1866 and Jesse's death in 1882, they robbed countless banks and trains. Jesse James was surprisingly popular with the public. Some viewed him as a kind of Robin Hood figure. He had fought for the South in the Civil War, and many in Missouri still opposed the Union. In addition, the railroad companies were unpopular because they had bought up such large amounts of land.

In 1876, the gang attempted to rob a bank in Northfield, Missouri. The raid went horribly wrong, and three of the band were killed. After this, big rewards were on offer to anyone who stopped Jesse James. In the end, it was a member of his own gang who killed him. Jesse James was shot in the back by Bob Ford as he straightened a picture in his own home.

Jesse James in death after being shot by Bob Ford.

BUTCH CASSIDY

Butch Cassidy was another outlaw who robbed banks and trains. His real name was Robert Leroy Parker, and he was born in 1866. His parents were Mormons. His gang was called the Wild Bunch, or the Hole in the Wall Gang. Harry Longbaugh, otherwise known as the Sundance Kid, who was born in 1861, was another member of the band.

The Wild Bunch targeted Union Pacific trains in Wyoming and Montana. One train was blown up so badly that $30,000 worth of notes lay scattered across the range. Pursued by Pinkerton detectives and other lawmen, Cassidy and the Sundance Kid emigrated to South America. They were killed in Bolivia in around 1908.

The Wild Bunch. The Sundance Kid is on the far left and Butch Cassidy is on the far right.

BILLY THE KID

Of all the Western celebrities, none has aroused more controversy than Billy the Kid. To some he was merely an outlaw, but others said that he fought against injustice. He was born Henry McCarty in 1859, although he often used the name William Bonney. He was only 17 when he first killed a man.

In 1878, a feud developed between two rival groups of ranchers in New Mexico. This was known as the Lincoln County War. Billy the Kid supported the side led by John Tunstall and John Chisum. They were challenging another group, led by Lawrence Murphy, for economic and political control of the area. Chisum and Tunstall believed that they were being denied their fair share of local trade and government beef contracts. Many killings followed. Billy the Kid was convicted of the murder of Sheriff Brady, one of Murphy's supporters. He escaped from prison, only to be shot dead by Sheriff Pat Garrett at Fort Sumner in 1881.

Billy the Kid. Contrary to popular belief, he was not left-handed.

BELLE STARR

Belle Starr's dramatic life caught the public imagination when she began to be featured in dime novels after her death. The books made a big feature of her appearance (she rode around in a plumed hat and velvet skirt).

Belle Starr's real name was Myra Belle Shirley, and she was born in 1848. She was the daughter of business people from Missouri. Throughout her life, she was associated with gunmen and outlaws. The father of her first child was said to be Cole Younger, who rode with the James gang. Both her husbands, James Reed and Sam Starr, were also outlaws. Belle Starr organised many crimes. She successfully avoided capture until she was eventually sentenced to nine months for horse stealing. Like many outlaws, she met a violent death, shot in the back by an unknown killer.

Belle Starr in her trademark plumed hat.

CALAMITY JANE

Calamity Jane's real name was Martha Jane Cannary (sometimes spelled 'Canary'), and she was born in 1852. With some Western figures, it is hard to separate myth from reality, and this is certainly true of her.

Martha Jane Cannary, alias Calamity Jane.

It is claimed that she joined the US army as a scout, only to be dismissed when she was discovered to be a woman. Whatever the truth of this, she was well known as a hard-drinking woman who often wore male clothes. She is most closely associated with Deadwood, and many films show her as being romantically involved with, or even married to, Wild Bill Hickok, but this is probably another Western myth. In later years, she went into show business, promoting her image as a frontierswoman. She died of pneumonia in 1903.

>> **Activities**

1 What were the causes of violence and lawlessness in the West?

2 How did the US government try to impose law and order in the West?

3 Use the biographies in this investigation to explain why outlaws

   a were often also lawmen;

   b became seen as heroes.

The Johnson County War

Today, the state of Wyoming is a quiet and law-abiding part of the USA. In 1892, Johnson County was the scene of a violent conflict between rich cattle owners and homesteaders. This was known as the Johnson County War.

What were the causes of the Johnson County War?

Homesteaders and the cattle industry

In the 1870s and early 1880s, many so-called cattle barons made fortunes out of the beef trade. The cattle boom was over by the end of the 1880s, and this was largely because of overproduction and the blizzards of 1886 and 1887. The big cattle ranchers did not see it this way. They blamed the decline on the small ranchers and homesteaders who, they claimed, had destroyed the open range by fencing in the land with barbed wire.

The situation became particularly tense in Johnson County, Wyoming. In this area, big ranchers had organised together as part of the Wyoming Stock Growers' Association, which was very powerful. The Johnson County War was an attempt by the cattle kings of the association to force the smaller ranchers and homesteaders out of the area.

Wyoming became a state in 1890, and it was dominated by the Republican Party. The governor was a Republican, as were the majority of the state senators. The cattlemen strongly supported the Republican Party. Most of the settlers, on the other hand, were Democrats or Populists (another political party of the time). Thus the Johnson County War was not only a case of large landowners against homesteaders; it also had a political aspect.

SOURCE A

The Wyoming Stock Growers' Association controlled Johnson County:

The stockmen have dominated the political and financial policy of the territory. The Wyoming Stock Growers' Association was a strong, centralized power, and for years virtually shaped the territorial policy. They dominated everywhere.

Asa Shinn Mercer, *Banditti of the Plains*, 1894

The Maverick Bill

The cattlemen suspected that many of the homesteaders were rustlers. There was some truth in this. Some small farmers and cowboys saw nothing wrong with taking unbranded steers. This gave the big ranchers an excuse to put pressure on the state to pass a local law known as the Maverick Bill in 1888. Under the terms of this new law, only the wealthy members of the Wyoming Stock Growers' Association were allowed to brand calves. Anyone else who tried to do this would be guilty of a crime.

Under the terms of the Bill, rich ranchers were allowed to take any unbranded calf found on the range. Thousands of cattle belonging to small farmers were seized. There was a great outcry. Newspapers took up the cause of the settlers, and protested about the actions of the association. The association appointed a former sheriff of Johnson County, Frank Canton, as its chief investigator. Canton was a lawman with a criminal past; he had been a bank robber and a rustler.

Violence against the settlers

The violence became worse. In 1889, two homesteaders, Jim Averill and Ella Watson, became the victims of vigilantes, and they were found hanged. It was widely thought that the culprit was Albert Bothwell, a big cattleman, because he claimed that he owned their land, and after the murders he took it.

The cattlemen continued their campaign. More murders occurred in 1891. Another settler, Nate Champion, who was accused of being a rustler, successfully defended himself against a lynching attempt.

The Johnson County Regulators in 1892. Some were local cattlemen; many were Texan gunfighters. None of them were brought to trial.

The cattlemen became bolder, and they launched an all-out assault on the settlers. They hired a group of over 50 men called the Regulators who were, in effect, a private army. Half of the men were gunfighters from Texas. The Regulators had a death list of over 60 names, including those of Nate Champion and Sheriff Red Angus, who had supported the settlers.

The death of Nate Champion

On 8 April 1892, news reached the Regulators that Nate Champion and a friend called Nick Ray were staying in a log cabin. The armed men reached the cabin on the following day. They surrounded the building, firing repeatedly. Nick Ray was the first to die. The Regulators decided to set fire to the cabin. Nate Champion made a dash for a ravine, where he was gunned down.

SOURCE C

Nate Champion (second left) was hailed as a hero after his death.

SOURCE D

Amazingly, Champion managed to keep a diary in a memo book during the siege of the cabin. He described the scene and his friend's death:

They are still shooting and are all around the house. Boys, there is bullets coming in like hail. The fellows is in such shape, I can't get at them. They are shooting from stable and river and back of the house. Nick is dead. He died about 9 o'clock. I see a smoke down at the stable. I think they have fired it. I don't think they intend to let me get away this time.

L. I. Seidman, *Once in the Saddle*, 1973

SOURCE E

The cabin where Nate Champion and Nick Ray fought so bravely before meeting their deaths.

SOURCE F

A popular ballad of the time told the story of Champion's death:

They've shot another volley in, but to burn me is their game,
And as I write, it's not yet night, and the house is all aflame.
So good-bye boys, if I get shot, I got to make a run,
So on this leaf I'll sign my name, Nathan D. Champion.

The light is out, the curtain drawn, the last sad act is played.
You know the fate that met poor Nate, and of the run he made.
And now across the Big Divide, and at the Home Ranch door,
I know he'll meet and warmly greet the boys that went before.

From 'The Ballad of Nate Champion'

L. I. Seidman, *Once in the Saddle*, 1973

Many people were outraged by news of the death of Ray and Champion. A merchant called Robert Foote organised opposition to the Regulators under the slogan 'Wyoming has been invaded'. Hundreds of people armed themselves and pursued the cattlemen and their allies, who took refuge in a ranch. They were surrounded by settlers, and the two sides battled it out for two days. On 12 April, US federal troops arrived, and the Regulators were released into the hands of the authorities. The Johnson County War was over.

The aftermath of the Johnson County War

In one sense, the cattlemen got off lightly. Neither they nor any of the Regulators were ever brought to court. The case against them was dropped. In the long term, though, it was a different matter. The cattle kings were never so powerful again, and the Republican Party lost control of the state at the next election.

>> Activities

1 What happened in the Johnson County War?

2 Was the conflict between cattle barons and homesteaders inevitable? Explain your answer using the information in this investigation.

The last days of the Wild West

THE JOHNSON COUNTY WAR

> Johnson County, Wyoming, was a centre of the cattle industry, which was dominated by large cattle barons and the Wyoming Stock Growers' Association.

> The cattle barons blamed the small ranchers and settlers in the area for the decline of the industry in the late 1880s. They suspected many of them of cattle rustling, and they wanted to force them out of the county.

> The cattle barons, who were Republican supporters, pressurised the Republican state government into passing the Maverick Bill in 1888. This was an attempt to prevent homesteaders from owning cattle, and it attracted great resentment.

> The murders of James Averill and Ella Watson in 1889 showed how far the cattle kings would go to protect their interests.

> The barons hired a group of gunmen called the Regulators to terrorise the settlers. In 1892, the settler Nate Champion bravely resisted the gunmen and was killed by them. He became a hero to many of the local people.

> The settlers fought back and the Regulators were trapped in a ranch. They had to be rescued by the federal authorities. Afterwards, none of the Regulators or cattle barons were convicted of any crime, but the cattle kings were never as powerful again.

LAW AND ORDER

> The West was probably not as wild as it has been made out to be, but there were law and order problems in the early days.

> Some areas were settled very quickly before strong government could be put in place. Decisions about the territories had to be taken by the distant federal government in Washington DC, and this could cause delays. The enormous extent of the West made it difficult to govern.

> Owners of large companies, such as the cattle barons, often resorted to violence to protect their interests. Ruthless individuals just took what they wanted.

> Sheriffs and marshals were sometimes unsuitable people for the job; some had a history of crime and violence.

> Vigilante attacks and lynchings were common. Miners, in particular, often resorted to vigilante justice.

>> Review question

Was the West in the nineteenth century really the 'Wild West'?

Index